*The*
# PETER TOWNSEND
*Story*

Peter Townsend

# The
# PETER
# TOWNSEND
## Story

### BY NORMAN BARRYMAINE

NEW YORK
E. P. DUTTON & CO., INC.
*1958*

Library of Congress Catalog Card No. 58-10823

American Book–Stratford Press, Inc., New York

# CONTENTS

# ILLUSTRATIONS

*The*
# PETER TOWNSEND
*Story*

# Introduction

In 1953—THE YEAR OF PETER TOWNSEND'S EXILE TO BELGIUM
—I was working in the Foreign Office in London. One morning in August I had a telephone call from Sir Christopher
Warner, our Ambassador in Brussels. He asked me if I could
come over the next weekend to discuss what he described as
"a private matter." He said it had nothing to do with my
official work.

I had been a friend of Christopher for twenty-five years
and a year earlier he had been my chief in the Foreign Office.
So I readily agreed to go and see him.

When I arrived in Brussels it was to find a rather vexed
Christopher. He said he wanted to talk to me about the
Margaret-Townsend affair. And added that he was very an-
noyed because Peter had been posted to his Embassy without the Foreign Office's first informing him. The appointment had been made while Christopher was on a visit to the
Belgian Congo, and the first he knew of his new Air Attaché
was from a paragraph in a Leopoldville newspaper.

It did not surprise me that Christopher had invited me to
Brussels to talk about the affair. I had been in his confidence
for a great many years and in the past he had often relied on
me for information because as a political journalist I had
many influential contacts in London and the other capitals
of the world.

When I made this first of many visits to Brussels, I had
met Peter only once before and that was very early in the
war.

My real association with Peter did not begin until early
in 1956 when he was planning his journey round the world.
He sought my advice on writing about his experiences.

Much has been written about Peter's romance with the Princess but the salient facts have never been revealed. I feel that it is important that they should be widely known because they involved important Constitutional, political, and religious problems. Princess Margaret's decision has a place in history. The reasons for reaching that decision are matters of vital public interest, and therefore open to discussion in our own country and the countries of the Commonwealth. The Princess' decision was not a *private* matter. It affected every one of her sister's subject peoples.

Some may think—and with justification—when they have read this book that modification of the law is desirable. That premise alone, in my opinion, justifies my having written what must prove to be a controversial work.

When I reached my decision last year to tell the Margaret-Townsend Story, I wrote to Peter, who was then driving across the Andes. I received a letter in reply which was typical of the man. This is what he said.

He objected to the writing of such a book on the grounds that it would bring him back into the middle of a controversy about the past. Further, he thought that the publicity the book would receive might prove an embarrassment to a number of people. Finally, he wished at all costs to avoid being party to any special pleading on his behalf to alter the decision of 1955, with which he was unmistakably associated.

Nevertheless, he said, he must be realistic, and he could not stop me from writing the book if I had made up my mind to do so. He appreciated my offer to let him see the manuscript before it went to the printers.

Peter has read the book—up to and including the events of 1955—and has corrected inaccuracies concerning his family and his life in the Royal Air Force but he has made *no comment* on his days as an Equerry at Buckingham Palace or his relations with Princess Margaret.

When I embarked on this book I knew that it was a story which Peter would never write himself, and, of course, it could not be written by the Princess. But when Peter said he could not stop me from writing it, he may have known that sooner or later someone with less knowledge of the facts would attempt such a work and, therefore, he might prefer me to be the author.

N. B.

Chequers,
Pulborough,
Sussex.
July, 1958.

# *Prologue*

It happened on june 2, 1953, coronation day—a day of national rejoicing.

Inside the Great Hall of the Annex to Westminster Abbey —a fabulous foyer with tapestry-draped walls and a cerise ceiling illumined with myriad silver stars—it was the hour of high drama.

Queen Elizabeth the Second had been crowned.

From the robing room which she was sharing with the Queen Mother came Princess Margaret. Anxiously she looked for one person amidst the richly robed company absorbed in conversation about the impressive, memorable ceremony they had just witnessed or the dramatic news of that morning of Hillary's conquest of Everest.

For minutes the Princess scanned the scene. Then, suddenly, her eyes fell on a young Group Captain in his sky-blue Royal Air Force uniform and *aiguillettes*—the gold lanyard and tassels worn on the right shoulder by the Equerries to the Queen.

Group Captain Peter Townsend's eyes caught sight of the Princess. They moved through the throng toward each other. As they drew near, the Princess' white gloved hands rested for a second on the Group Captain's chest. There was a cotton thread on the breast pocket. Gently, the Princess took off the offending thread, and then, with infinite care, brushed the bemedaled tunic with her gloved hand. For seconds they stood there, not talking—just looking into each other's eyes.

The great bells of Westminster Abbey were pealing. Music swelled from the Abbey organ, enveloping the Hall. But Princess Margaret and Group Captain Townsend were unaware of all this drama. They were alone in splendid com-

15

pany. They were alone with their love and for a few seconds they did not care if the world knew.

Nor was this the last time that they were alone together that day. That night they mingled unnoticed among the thousands who thronged the Mall and massed around the statue of Queen Victoria, calling for their Queen. The jostling cheering crowd never recognized the two familiar figures in their midst.

The Princess and her Group Captain had slipped out of a side gate to Buckingham Palace. As they threaded their way under the illuminated triumphal arches, they met Princess Alexandra of Kent.

"What are you doing here?" she asked.

"Just looking, the same as you," replied Princess Margaret. "After all, we're the Queen's subjects too."

A week or two later, Group Captain Peter Townsend was posted to Brussels as Air Attaché at the British Embassy.

Princess Margaret and Peter Townsend have never again been lost together in a crowd.

# The Airman

ONE NIGHT IN FEBRUARY, 1940, WHEN THE "PHONY" WAR
was still on, an intensely excited and exuberant young man
was performing a wild dance in the mess of a Royal Air
Force station in Northern England. His partner was Flight
Lieutenant Caesar Hull, a very brave uninhibited South
African, who was later to die in the Battle of Britain.

The excited young man was Peter Wooldridge Townsend.

No. 43 Fighter Squadron, twenty-four years old and one
of the most famous of the Royal Air Force, was celebrating.
Peter Townsend, Caesar Hull, and John Simpson had that
day each shot down a Heinkel bomber attacking fishing boats
off the northeast coast.

Against the picture of Hurricane fighters closing in on the
Heinkels with that fatal rasping stutter of machine guns, and
the later party in the mess with champagne corks popping
and Peter and Caesar performing their improvised Spanish
dance, emerges the portrait of Peter Townsend, then a Flight
Lieutenant.

I met Townsend for the first time that night. (Sixteen
years were to pass before we met again.) I had flown north
from Fighter Command Headquarters at Stanmore in Mid-
dlesex to interview him, Hull, and Simpson. Peter's "kill"
that day was an event. His Heinkel was the first German
bomber to be shot down on English soil.

World War II was a high point in Peter Townsend's life
and it set the pattern of his future outlook and conduct. He
was among the gayest and bravest of the airmen and he was
decisively formed by those soul-shaping war experiences that
a man can register only once in a lifetime.

Peter Townsend is a finely strung man, who has spent most

17

of his life getting what he wants. Often he does it with a splash. Even as a child his small mobile features drew attention wherever they were seen. He grew up to be like the typical sixth-form hero of schoolboy fiction: the good-looking, gay lad who is perfect at whatever he does and makes it all seem easy and casual, who leads without ostentatiously exercising authority, whose actions often contain an element of drama, and who is worshiped by the small fry.

Yet Peter Townsend is a man of complex character—a deeply religious fighter who hated what he did in the war, yet did it because he knew he had to, a man extremely conscious of his duty at all times. Above all, perhaps, a man of infinite charm and ability who appeals, on first acquaintance, to women more than men. Women, though, seldom mention his masculinity. Said one: "Peter reminds me of a Siamese cat. He is so fastidious." Said another: "He is considerate and attentive. He never forgets a thing. He has a way of never letting a minute be boring."

Physically, Peter Townsend is handsome, but not in the husky style of a professional athlete or film star. In a crowd, even were he unknown, he would stand out as being "different." Five feet eleven inches tall, he is slim with powerful shoulders, has a fine face, a firm pointed chin, and a sensitive nose which is perilously close to being too long. His blue-gray eyes appear to be looking into the distance. His smile is diffident and quizzical, as though he were surprised at the interest in what he has to say. His hands are honest and strong. And yet they are gentle hands.

Someone once compared him to a shy Gregory Peck. One of his prewar acquaintances recalls that, just before the war, she traveled back to Britain from Palestine on the same ship with Townsend. They did not meet during the voyage, but years later, when she was a WAAF assistant section officer at the fighter station where Townsend was second in command, he entranced her by saying when they were introduced:

"Surely we have met before. I seem to remember your face set against a blue sea."

Men who were with him during the war recall that he was uncommonly reserved. Peter had, and still has, the delicate sensitiveness of the man who is not entirely sure of himself and, more important, of his power over other people.

Some of his acquaintances have looked upon him as a little cold. Others have mistaken his shyness and his look of often intense concentration for haughtiness. But all agree on one point. Townsend has a knack of getting his own way most of the time. A man who served under him when he was Equerry to King George VI recalled: "Townsend never gave a direct order. He always said: 'Would you mind very much doing this?' or 'Do you think it would be a good thing? . . .'"

Even today, in his loneliness, he has not lost his immense charm, his gaiety, his wit, and a flow of high spirits. He continues to be excellent company and stimulating. But the steadiness of his blue eyes suggests for all their gaiety and charm that here is a man a little withdrawn into himself.

The truth is that Peter wears the aura of a man who fought with The Few in the sense of Winston Churchill's phrase.

The world has not heard the last of Peter Townsend.

Townsend's father, Lieutenant Colonel Edward Copleston Townsend, went to Haileybury, then into the Indian Army and the Burma Commission. He came from a Devon family, whose sons for generations have gone into the Church or the Services. In the family tree are a Surgeon-General of the Indian Army, a Royal Navy Captain, and several clergymen. A family, in fact, that has always served its country.

Peter was born in Rangoon on November 22, 1914, where his father was Commissioner of the Pegu Division, a member of the Legislative Council, and therefore one of the most senior representatives of the Crown in what was then part of the Indian Empire.

Peter was the fifth of seven children—Audrey, Michael,

Philip, Juliet, Peter, Stephanie, and Francis. All the Town-send sons, except Francis, chose military careers. All have done well.

Philip is a Brigadier of the Gurkha Rifles. He fought in Burma during the war, has been in Malaya during the last two years, and holds the Distinguished Service Order.

Michael, a crisp yet soft-spoken Rear Admiral in the Royal Navy, also had a brilliant war career. He distinguished him-self as a destroyer commander; he was awarded the D.S.O., D.S.C., and bar, and the Order of the British Empire.

Francis, the youngest son, was at Wellington when the war broke out, but toward the end of the war chose to go into the R.A.F. After the war he went to Oxford and then into the Colonial Service. He is now a District Commissioner of the Masai in Tanganyika. Francis met Princess Margaret when she visited East Africa—at the Princess' request.

All the daughters have made good marriages. Tall elegant Stephanie married Arthur Gaitskell, the brother of Hugh Gaitskell, the leader of the Labour Party. They have three children.

The two older daughters are Audrey and Juliet. Audrey, who won a scholarship to Oxford, is the wife of Commander C. J. O. Malcolm, R.N. retired, headmaster of a preparatory school for boys at Hawkhurst, near Cranbrook, Kent.

Juliet married Deryck Flint, a partner in a London firm of chartered surveyors.

Peter, with his sister Juliet, was brought back to England by his mother from Burma in April, 1915. He was then only five months old. The brother and sister were left with an aunt, and Mrs. Townsend returned to her husband in Ran-goon. In 1917, Colonel Townsend retired, and came home to England with his wife.

In due course young Peter was sent to his father's old school, Haileybury College, twenty miles north of London. Though not as upper-crust as Eton or as intellectual as Win-chester, Haileybury is scholastically respectable and sufficiently bleak to convince the civil servants, stockbrokers, army and navy officers, and other middle-class types who are graduated from it that they have not been spared any of the advantages or rigors of public school life.

It must have been quite a financial strain on Townsend's father to send him there, but Colonel Townsend and his wife, the former Miss Hatt-Cook whom he married in 1906, made great sacrifices for their large family. Mrs. Gladys Townsend, a gentle, gray-haired lady now in her seventies, who still loves to drive her eight-horsepower car, now lives in Stogumber, near Taunton, in the heart of the rolling Quantook Hills of Somerset. Near her, in the adjoining village of Bicknoller, are the homes of Stephanie and her husband, and Philip, the Brigadier, and his wife and family.

Peter was only twelve when he took the Common Entrance examination for Haileybury. He passed second and for two terms was the youngest boy in the school.

Before going to Haileybury he was at a preparatory school in Bournemouth. The Headmaster, the Reverend H. M. Batley, was a good cricketer and he had a fondness for Peter, probably because he showed great promise as a bat.

Something of Peter's character began to emerge when he went to Haileybury. He was intensely shy and very nervous. The Reverend Batley probably was confident that Peter would play cricket for his school. But, in fact, he touched a bat only once while he was at Haileybury.

The reason was a strange one—the more so when one knows that this was the boy who when he reached his twenties was to fight with such courage and determination in the Battle of Britain.

A day or so after reaching Haileybury, he went out to the new "Gu'nor" nets like all the new boys to see if he had any promise. Peter was trembling from head to foot, and, in fact, was so nervous that he couldn't hit a ball. He was promptly declared "useless."

So he stopped playing cricket, and yet he still has a deep appreciation of the game.

He took up swimming and was captain of swimming for three years. He also played rugby in the First Fifteen as scrum half.

He was an above the average student at Haileybury. Mathematics did not come easy to him but he was good in Latin and French, and, in the tradition of sensitive boys, fond of reading poetry in and out of school hours. When he sat for his school certificate, he failed in maths—much to his father's disgust. He also did very badly in Scripture being given 8 out of 100 and 13 out of a 100 in two papers. "The examiners apparently thought my theology a little too original." In view of Peter's later feeling for the Scriptures these low marks were surprising.

Peter became a prefect and was head of his house, Lawrence. His name is carved in the oak panels that record the school teams, and written in gilt in his house along with the other heads of Lawrence.

Somewhat ironically, in view of the consternation he was to cause in later years in royal and ecclesiastical circles, his school motto was: Fear God, Honor the King. It will be seen later that in the hour of decision he did not forget those words, and what they meant.

Just before Peter took his entrance examination to the Royal Air Force College at Cranwell he suffered a concussion while playing rugby. In the examination he passed fifth, thus gaining a cadetship, but failed his medical. But on his second attempt he passed the medical and was fourth in the examination and thus once more qualified for a cadetship.

Peter chose the Air Force as a career because of a burning desire to fly. His father, perhaps, would have preferred him to have chosen the Indian Forestry Service.

It was August 31, 1933, when he went to Cranwell. His Commandant was Philip Babington who thought that Peter possessed all the qualities to be awarded the coveted Sword of Honor. And, yet, Peter was not always prepared to work in the somewhat monotonous routine of Cranwell life. But he was a brilliant pilot, being one of the first of his class to fly solo when still only eighteen. He had only six hours "dual" before doing so.

The course at Cranwell was two years and in the last six months Peter became very impatient. One day he was invited to tea by Babington. Peter inquired discreetly if any other cadets were going. When he found that he was to be the only guest, he knew that the invitation was not for a purely social visit. Peter's intuition was correct.

Over the teacups Babington was charming and friendly but at the same time brutally frank with Peter. He had hoped he would win the Sword of Honor. But Peter, he said, was a "rebel." He made the criticism almost affectionately, pointing out there had to be "rebels in the world."

In his last term Peter was one of the three squadron-under-officers at the College. Babington assessed him as a man of "initiative and courage." Peter asked to be posted to the No. 1 fighter squadron at Tangmere, one of the three crack interceptor squadrons in what was then called Fighting Area. His wish was granted.

In the summer of 1935 he found himself for the first time at Tangmere, which nestled below the Sussex Downs. Eight months later he was posted to No. 36 Squadron in Singapore. This squadron was equipped with out-of-date Vildebeest torpedo bombers. In the cockpit was a solemn notice: NOT TO BE FLOWN AT A SPEED IN EXCESS OF 140 MILES AN HOUR. Five years later every one of these aircraft was lost in a low-level attack on the Japanese fleet off the coast of Malaya.

For Peter, the years in Singapore were happy days. He especially enjoyed a 9,000-mile flight from Singapore to the Northwest Frontier and back. Under the command of Squadron Leader Peter Davies, himself something of a "rebel," the squadron made the flight and back without any casualties, the only time this was ever achieved.

While Peter was in Singapore he was invited like all other young officers to specialize in one of five subjects: armament, engineering, signals, navigation, or photography. Peter discarded these and chose to study languages. He had a choice of Japanese, Chinese, Arabic, Kurdish, and Russian. As he was greatly interested in the Far East, it was natural for him to select Japanese. But later he had second thoughts. When he reached England he disregarded normal procedure and requested that he should be permitted to study Russian. This was granted and he was put down for a course to begin in 1941.

While Peter was at Cranwell, he had suffered with skin trouble, and in Singapore he had a recurrence that affected both arms. He went to seek advice from Dr. Young of the School of Tropical Medicine in Singapore. Young carried out a long series of allergy tests—from petrol to bananas, all of which proved negative.

Young said there was only one cure: Peter must stop flying—forever. "You must live like a cabbage for a while," added the doctor.

"But flying is my life," protested Peter. "If I stop flying I have nothing to live for."

Young went to the R.A.F. medical officer in Singapore and urged that Peter be sent home. In May, 1937, he sailed for England.

Peter had one lucky escape from death just before he left Singapore. One afternoon he was cleaning his midget blue M.G. sports car outside the mess at Seletar. He stopped and went indoors to get another duster. When he came out a few minutes later he found that the rear fender which he had been polishing was cut away. It had been hit by a trailing aerial which a Vildebeest navigator had forgotten to wind in when his pilot signaled he was landing.

On the voyage home Peter's skin trouble cleared up and

when he went before the R.A.F. Central Medical Board in London he was passed as fit. In fact, the doctors could not understand why he had been sent home. Peter was a little apprehensive about going back to flying but he had no alternative in face of the Board's decision.

He was posted again to Tangmere, this time to the crack 43rd Squadron, formed in World War I by the man who is now Lord Douglas, Chairman of British European Airways.

Within a few weeks of resuming flying, Peter's skin trouble returned. Now he was convinced that his complaint, which today would be diagnosed as neurodermatitis, was caused by flying. Why should this be? He loved flying. But doubts were beginning to creep into his mind as to whether he wished to remain in the Air Force. Peter seldom talks about those days even to his most intimate friends. They were soul-searching days. What was the question that was haunting him? Could he kill, if war came? And war seemed certain.

By the end of 1937 he had reached a decision. He would leave the Royal Air Force. Before sending in his resignation he went to see Philip Babington, to whom he was devoted. They had a long talk. Babington, who understood the complexities of character of this young man whom two years before he had called a "rebel," was able to dissuade Peter from resigning.

Perhaps because of Babington's intervention, Peter was sent early in 1938 on a four-months navigation course at the School of Air Navigation at Manston. His health improved. After this he spent a few months with a general reconnaissance squadron but he yearned to be back with a fighter unit. In the end his wish was granted and he was posted back again to 43 Squadron. This move earned him the reputation among his fellow pilots of being a "fixer." To get back to fighters, he had said somewhat disingenuously that being flown by someone else made him nervous and that it would probably bring back his skin trouble.

But even after he was posted back to 43 Squadron he was still in doubt about his future.

Under the threat of Hitler, the Royal Air Force was beginning to expand and its character was changing. The new Air Force did not appeal to Peter's temperament. He felt it was becoming too big for his individualism. But by the time of Munich in the autumn of 1938, even if his doubts still lingered, there was no turning back. Above all, Peter is a man of great courage. Yet he is not without fear. That makes his fighting career even more courageous and magnificent.

But the Peter of the Battle of Britain was then unborn.

At the time of Munich, morale among the fighter pilots was not at its best, primarily because of the poor fighting qualities of their aircraft—no match for Goering's Heinkel bombers—but partly because some of the senior officers could not conceal their depression. It affected the young men.

Munich, however, brought not war but peace—at least temporarily. And three months later, to the joy of all in 43 Squadron, their slow-moving planes were replaced with the fast-flying Hawker Hurricane—the fighter, together with the Spitfire, that was to decimate Goering's bombers in 1940.

Morale in 43 Squadron jumped sky-high. And probably because of the influence of the other pilots, any doubts which Peter had had a few months before disappeared. His skin trouble had not returned.

We know what Peter was like in those days from the letters of John Simpson to Hector Bolitho. Simpson wrote:

"Yes, it was Peter Townsend I meant. He used to be rather aloof, going to his room at night and avoiding our games and parties. But we are bringing him out of his shell. He is very shy and has no idea of his courage. He thinks he will hate war if it comes. Caesar moans because there is no war. He reads Winston Churchill by the hour and knows all the answers. Peter is a different type. Very English on the surface. His brothers are in the Navy and Army and he was in torpedo bombers in the Far East. He's the greatest gentleman I have ever met in the Service. He surrounds himself with armor, but I am slowly breaking through. We are becoming friends. You will like him when you know him more. He's got the sort of face you notice immediately he comes into a room."

If Peter, during those months before the outbreak of war in 1939, became more mentally stable and gained a new confidence, it was owing almost entirely to one man—Caesar Hull, perhaps the greatest fighter pilot of the war.

Peter never tries to hide what he owes to Caesar. "He really taught me to fly," he once said. Peter was an introvert. Caesar was a massive extrovert. Together they defied all the rules. But if they appeared to do foolhardy stunts, like flying wingtip to wing-tip at the white cliffs of Dover and then pulling up at the last split second to see who got frightened first, they both kept in a state of superb physical fitness. They trained like boxers for a world championship fight.

Townsend still likes to talk of those halcyon days—days of spiritual freedom for Peter and Caesar, although neither of them at the time defined it that way.

# One of The Few

THEN CAME THE WAR. ALL THE PILOTS OF 43 SQUADRON WERE at Dispersal Point at Tangmere when Neville Chamberlain announced in a weary voice on the wireless at 11 o'clock on the morning of September 3, 1939, that Britain's ultimatum to Hitler, head of the Third Reich, had expired and that the country was at war with Germany for a second time in the century. The pilots, lying in the sunshine on the grass, listened intently to their portable radios until the Prime Minister finished speaking.

Within a few minutes of the end of the broadcast there was an alert. At that moment an aeroplane was flying across the Channel toward the south coast of England.

For the first time since 1918, sirens howled. The wail of the banshee, as Winston Churchill afterward called it.

The aeroplane was moving toward London. But just south of the capital it began to circle. It came down at Croydon. Two French officers—a captain and lieutenant—stepped out. They were on their way to join the Allied air mission in London.

The "raiders passed" signal wailed. The Frenchmen looked puzzled. Had the Germans perhaps, already? . . . An R.A.F. officer laughed and explained. The captain and the lieutenant were apologetic.

The first "air raid" of the war was over.

Not a very satisfactory morning in the eyes of George Lott, Commander, and Peter, Caesar, John, and the other young pilots of 43 Squadron.

This is not my story, but I was able, in the Operations Room of Commander-in-Chief Air Chief Marshal Sir Hugh Dowding's headquarters at Fighter Command, to watch the growth of the battle, even if it was only on maps and in reports. We felt part of a miracle when we read the combat reports, reports from men so tired they could barely write. They wrote their stories of heroism in phrases as simple as the Psalms. And, like the Psalms, they seemed to come from another world.

For the first few months of the war Peter and his fellow pilots never got a glimpse of the enemy. Then they were moved from Tangmere to Acklington air base on the northeast coast and given the mission of defending from the air a coastal belt stretching five miles out to sea. They settled down to their first job of fighting. They had expected to take the air against heavy formations of the *Luftwaffe*, threatening the country's cities and factories. Instead they became shipping guards, patrolling the coast during all the hours of daylight, circling high above the shore-hugging convoys, driving a slowly mounting score of Heinkels and Dorniers one by one into the sea.

To them it was monotonous work. But the Germans were giving them unexpected and valuable training under war conditions. Pilots who had patrolled over the North Sea in all weathers, shooting down single raiders that were as difficult to find as a rabbit flea on a mountainside, knew what to do when they met German bombers and fighters in their scores and hundreds over Dunkirk and the English Channel and London.

During the first eight months of the war, up to the invasion of Holland and Belgium, the fighter pilots in their Spitfires and Hurricanes were defending a goal 1,000 miles wide and 5 or 6 miles high against three kinds of enemy—the single reconnaissance machine which, usually with fine navigational skill, made photographic flights over Britain; the raiders which tried to bomb and machine-gun fishing vessels, merchantmen, and even lightships; and, thirdly, the seaplanes which flew over at night to drop their magnetic mines in the estuaries and harbor mouths.

To keep that goal these pilots were flying by April, 1940, 2,000,000 miles a month. That would not, perhaps, seem an excessive mileage for a force of long-distance bombers or flying boats, but the average patrol of a Spitfire or Hurricane in those days did not last more than an hour. To fly 2,000,000 miles a month (equal to more than 3,000 flights to Berlin) Fighter Command had to send up, during the latter part of this period, some 220 Spitfires and Hurricanes a day. Yet from the outbreak of war until the Dunkirk battles, not a single pilot was lost in battle. Two were slightly wounded. One, shot down into the sea, lost the only fighter aircraft, a Spitfire, that the enemy could claim over the British coasts in eight months.

All told until the opening of the Norwegian campaign in the spring, some 40-odd German bombers were destroyed out of some 400 reported over or near British shores—no mean task for fighters operating at the fringe of their interception system against bombers attacking widely dispersed targets.

Peter's squadron flew hundreds of sorties. They destroyed six Heinkel 111 bombers. Peter made two "kills" himself.

Caesar Hull brought down the first enemy aircraft for his squadron. Thirteen days later, on January 30, 1940, the three friends, Caesar, John, and Peter, came into their own as fighter pilots. They were the leaders of three sections that brought down three German bombers, within the space of five minutes.

Peter Townsend and his "Blue" section were ordered off to patrol South Shields. Shortly afterward the sections commanded by Caesar Hull and John Simpson were ordered into the air—Caesar's three aircraft to patrol the mouth of the Tyne and John Simpson's section the Farne Islands. Operations Room had told them that there were enemy bombers about, presumably looking for convoys.

When Simpson landed, he thought he had drawn first blood. But Peter had gone in before him.

Peter with Flying Officer "Tiger" Folkes and Sergeant Hallowes intercepted a Heinkel three miles east of Whitby. While Hallowes headed the bomber off from escaping into cloud, Peter opened fire with Folkes following up the attack. Badly damaged, the Heinkel crashed near a farm in Yorkshire.

On the tarmac talking to John Simpson, Peter was excited but modest. He just said: "Poor devils, I don't think they were all killed."

As they were talking the news came over the radio-telephone that Caesar Hull and Frank Carey (he rose from the rank of Sergeant Pilot to Wing Commander in two years) had shot down a third near the mouth of the Tyne. They landed a few minutes later.

Caesar was frightfully excited, saying, "God! It was wizard! Frank and I did beam attacks from opposite directions and nearly collided."

That night, Peter and Caesar did their wonderful dance, *La Cachita,* to the record they had brought from Tangmere. The dance was a cross between a rumba and an apache dance, and Peter and Caesar threw each other all over the room with much crashing and banging. They jumped over the tables and chairs while they were dancing.

It was quite a party. They drank eight bottles of champagne. They sang old Air Force songs—"My mother comes from Norfolk" ... "Take the piston rings out of my stomach."

The next day Peter and Caesar went over to the farm at Whitby to see the wrecked Heinkel. Then they drove to the Whitby War Memorial hospital and took the German airman, Karl Missy, some cigarettes. One of his legs had been amputated.

Fifteen years later Peter was to meet Missy again. This time it was in Dusseldorf, where Townsend was taking part in a race. Karl was then forty-two and with an artificial leg.

Recalling the wartime meeting in the hospital, Karl Missy, in his home town of Rheyt, near Cologne, said: "I shall

never forget that the man who shot me down was my first
visitor in hospital. He was so full of gaiety and warmth of
feeling. First he patted me on the shoulder. Then he produced a bag of oranges and bananas from behind his back
and two packets of cigarettes. He sat at my bedside and we
tried to talk. It was difficult. I knew only a few words of
English and he very little German. But we managed. We
tried to talk about our jobs in the air. When language failed,
he straddled his chair to imitate an aeroplane seat and made
signs."

But that air battle in the winter of 1940 was a touch-and-
go affair for Peter Townsend. Gunner Missy had Townsend's Hurricane in his gunsight.

"I fired," says Missy, "and missed. Townsend fired and I
felt my legs crumple beneath me. We made a forced landing.
Two of the crew of four were dead."

Townsend's last words to him in the hospital were: "You're
a good boy. Get better soon."

When they met in the years after the war, Missy told
Townsend that he was a master plumber, married, and had a
four-year-old daughter. Before they parted Townsend and
Missy agreed that neither wanted war again "in any shape or
form."

All through the damp misty days of February, 1940, 43
Squadron went on with its dull and very tiring—they often
flew only a few feet off the tops of the waves—patrols in
defense of coastal convoys. And this patrol work was done
during the hardest winter in over forty years.

The days of 43 Squadron on the northeast coast, however,
were numbered.

Britain's main naval bases on the east coast needed protection. And Scapa Flow in the Orkney Islands, Scotland,
was the most difficult proposition, for it was far outside the
general Fighter Command system.

In spite of the severity of the weather and the remoteness

of the locality, the winter months saw the development of the fighter sector for the Orkneys pressed on apace.

Thus Peter Townsend and the other pilots of 43 Squadron found themselves early in 1940 transferred to Wick airfield, the farthermost point in Scotland.

But before 43 went north, Peter and Caesar demonstrated an aerial dance. 152 Squadron, which was sharing Acklington airfield, was equipped with Spitfires, and one day Peter and Caesar asked Freddy Shute, the C.O. of 152, to permit them to try out the Spits. They took off a few minutes after each other and circled the airfield, then joined formation. In view of the whole airfield, they did a loop and a roll, in close formation. They were not even content with this bit of "line shooting."

Caesar had invented an aerial version of the *La Cachita* dance. Calling out *La Cachita* to Peter over the R/t, followed with a noise like firing machine guns, Peter called back: *"Himmel, Himmel! Achtung! Schpitfeuer!"* Then they went into a mock air duel. By the time they had landed the Spitfires, after a demonstration of this dance, Freddy Shute was plenty angry.

Business up in Wick was at first pretty dull. But Peter and Caesar refused to take a day off in case anybody else got the Germans before them. When they were ordered off for a week's leave they were back in three days lest they miss something.

With the defenses of Scapa Flow strengthened in the air, on the ground, and under the water, early in March the Home Fleet, which had been moved to the west coast of Scotland, returned and the enemy stepped up its attacks on Scapa.

In one raid the *Luftwaffe* sent ten bombers. 43 Squadron intercepted the Heinkels ten miles off the Orkneys and as the Hurricane pilots said, "gave them hell!" At least five were shot down.

Peter and Caesar destroyed one bomber each in this battle. A few days later there was another "party"—to use the R.A.F. vernacular. Peter felt he had to write about it:

"It was the afternoon of a lovely day, April 10. The sky and the sea were very blue. There were scattered clouds and isolated rainstorms, none of which would give much cover to a snooper.

"Caesar's flight were released from duty and he and some others were playing tennis. My flight was at thirty minutes notice and was the last of five flights available for action. So I went into the town with Eddie to do some shopping.

"The siren was sounded just as we were buying some things. We ran to the aerodrome which was a mile away, and arrived at our dispersal hut, hot and flustered. George Lott was already there. He had been sitting in his office when he saw a lot of chaps rushing past the window. He had telephoned Ops. to see if there was anything doing. When they told him that there were some Huns about, he asked: 'Can we go?'

"Much to my annoyance we found that 'B' Flight had only three aircraft which were serviceable. Several had been damaged when we brought down the five Germans in the blitz off Scapa Flow.

"Then Caesar arrived, with some others in his flight—'A.' They were still wearing their tennis clothes—shirts, flannels, rubber shoes. There were only a few of their pilots as the others had gone off for the day. It was a case of my flight having the pilots and Caesar's having the machines. There was rather a heated discussion and then we arranged a com-promise.

"As we flew out towards the islands, we saw one Hun. We gave the 'Tallyho' in one bellow over the R/T. The Hun might have heard us, he turned so steeply away and made for a small bank of cloud. George Lott got there first and gave him a burst just before he got into the cloud. Then Caesar showed his independence. He opened the throttle full out and drew away from me. Then he tore into the Hun, who was then dodging in and out of the cloud. Now it was a matter of each man for himself.

"We jostled and dodged each other as we tore in behind the Heinkel and every now and then there would be a yell of 'Look out! For Christ's sake you nearly hit me.'

"I remember coming in with another Hurricane dangerously close above me.

"The rudder and fin of the Heinkel were wobbling and his whole fuselage was riddled. We told the boys not to fire any more because we saw that he was finished and we wanted, if possible, to bring them back alive.

"Caesar and I flew in close to him, one on each side, and I could see the horrible mess in the rear cockpit. It was a sad and beastly sight. But we were elated then and we did not see it that way. The riddled aircraft with its flapping *empennage,* three terrified figures in front of the aircraft. The pilot, his fair hair blown by the slipstream which was coming through his shattered windscreen, leaning forward and trying to urge his powerless machine to fly, his two companions making hopeless signs of surrender and despair. We just answered them with two fingers and an upturned thumb, as we pointed toward the coast which was thirty miles away, in the hope that they would make it. They didn't. The pilot brought his aircraft down to sea level and, pump-handling the control column, he brought the Heinkel to rest on the water. The fuselage broke in half immediately and the after end sank. One wing broke off and, tipping crazily in the air for a second, it slithered below the surface.

"Three figures struggled clear of the sinking wreckage. They began to swim *backstroke,* in that icy water, toward the coast. The seven of us circled round and some of us transmitted to get a wireless fix for our position, so that they might send out a launch to rescue the Huns. But none came.

"We resumed our formation and flew back. I can still see the agony and despair of the last minutes of those Huns. We were indifferent to it then, when we saw them. We knew quite well that many of us would have to endure just as much before the war finished."

On April 31, 1940, it was announced in the London *Gazette* that he had been awarded the Distinguished Flying Cross. The citation read:

"While on patrol over the North Sea, Flight Lieutenant Peter Townsend intercepted and attacked an enemy aircraft at dusk, and after a running fight, shot it down. This was his third success, and in each instance he displayed qualities of leadership, skill and determination of the highest order, with little regard for his own safety."

Soon afterward he went to Buckingham Palace to have the medal pinned on his breast by King George VI.

The ill-starred Norwegian campaign that started in April marked the end of the Townsend-Hull partnership and of the heroic part played by Caesar Hull—the pilot for whom "every night was guest night." Caesar did more than any other person to alter the course of Peter's life, for it was Caesar, I think, who "humanized" Peter. So perhaps a bit more about the man is in order.

The Allied units in Norway were desperately in need of fighter protection. It was decided to send 263 Squadron on board the aircraft carrier *Glorious*. This squadron was chosen because its obsolescent Gladiator biplanes could operate from small landing grounds. Caesar Hull had been transferred from 43 to 263 to take part in this hazardous operation.

The pilots of Squadron 263 landed their Gladiators on Lake Lesjakog in Norway without mishap, despite a heavy snowstorm. But the next day, ten of the eighteen Gladiators were put out of action on the ground, and by evening much of the squadron was destroyed.

Nothing remained but to withdraw the pilots in a cargo ship. They reached Scapa Flow safely on May 1—exactly ten days after they sailed to Norway from the same place.

The destruction of 263 Squadron meant the abandonment of the entire Central Norwegian project.

While Central Norway was witnessing the first of the evacuations of 1940 and 1941, the expedition in the north was in a fair way to success. Narvik was not within easy reach of enemy-held airfields.

Wing Commander R. L. R. Atcherley—known throughout the R.A.F. as "Batchy" Atcherley—was sent from England to prospect sites for landing grounds in the neighborhood of Narvik. Promising sites were found to be existing landing grounds at Bardufoss and Banak. There was no darkness when night came and Atcherley worked on with his men, day after day, until protecting bays had been built with fallen trees and the runways were in good shape.

Meanwhile 263 Squadron, with a fresh supply of Gladiators, sailed in the *Furious* on May 14, and had to spend some days waiting offshore while the final preparations were made at Bardufoss. On May 22, the Squadron established itself at Bardufoss and flew fifty sorties before the brief Arctic twilight called a halt to operations. Despite many handicaps, the Gladiators kept up a daily average of over forty sorties.

Caesar Hull, commanding one flight, was among those who got through safely. It was the first time that Atcherley had met Hull, but he had heard about the reputation of both Peter and Caesar in 43 Squadron. After the Norwegian campaign Atcherley wrote: "Caesar was a Hurricane in himself. He drank his life in quick gulps. He lacked all the textbook elements of leadership, completely unconscious of the qualities that made him so. He was frightfully good company. Colossal dash. Bold in the air and a cracking good shot. He had every single qualification that a man could have. He was effervescent but never bubbly. He was able and bloody brave. I don't think there was anything lacking in him. His leadership was based on excellence in everything."

At midday on May 26 three Gladiators took off from Bardufoss for Bodö, where a hastily prepared landing ground was now available for support of ground forces resisting the German advance north.

The leader of this section was Caesar.

During a German attack on Bodö, Caesar crashed and was wounded in the head and in one knee. Atcherley sent him back to England. In the hospital at home he recovered, and after spending sick leave in Guildford was back with 43. All that he could have ever wished for was his when he was given command of the squadron, and he led them in the Battle of Britain. On September 7—the height of the battle—he failed to return from a patrol off the Kentish coast.

The struggle for Norway was followed by the collapse in the West and Dunkirk.

With the collapse in the West, Winston Churchill made one of his historic and imperishable speeches, with this per-oration:

> "What General Weygand called the Battle of France is over. I expect that the Battle of Britain is about to begin. The whole fury and might of the enemy must very soon be turned on us. Hitler knows that he will have to break us in this island or lose the war. If we can stand up to him, all Europe may be free and the life of the world may move forward into broad sunlit uplands. But if we fail, then the whole world, including the United States, including all that we have known and cared for, will sink into the abyss of a new Dark Age made more sinister, and perhaps more protracted, by the lights of perverted science. Let us therefore brace ourselves to our duties, and so bear ourselves that, if the British Empire and its Commonwealth last for a thousand years, men will say, 'This was their finest hour.'"

Fighter Command, under the direction of Dowding, was preparing hastily for the new onslaught on the shores of Britain, and Peter was promoted. John Simpson wrote to Bolitho: "Caesar is still in Norway with 'Batchy' Atcherley. And now Peter has gone. I am pleased for him as he has done so well with us. I know he will be magnificent with a squadron of his own. He is an extraordinary person. Do you remember how shy and self-contained he was? It has all gone now. He loves his gay parties and the squadron worships him. He is the hero of the squadron to the ground staff. What a lesson one can learn from a person like that, in watching the way he works with the men. He never needs to be angry or tiresome, or even particularly firm with them. It just comes from inside him and I suppose they know a gentleman when they meet one. I have noticed it a lot when I have been censoring the men's letters, how they all think the world of him. I shall miss him. I'll bet he'll do the best for all of us in this bloody war."

But Peter, who had now had his first medal for gallantry pinned on his chest by the King, was if anything more tortured rather than elated by his victories over the enemy. Also, he was troubled as to what could come out of the war. I think all the fighter pilots in those days were troubled by doubts about the future. One heard in the messes continuous arguments—philosophic, political, and religious.

Peter was saying: "The only way a man can qualify for leadership is through personal example." Someone—an older officer—replied: "But you who survive the war must be the leaders of the peace—see that the right kind of world is built."

In King George VI, Peter was later to find a man who epitomized his dictum of "leadership through example." That is one reason why a friendship grew up between Monarch and Equerry.

At the end of May Peter was given command of 85 Squadron, which had been decimated by fighting against impossible odds in France since the outbreak of war. They had lost heavily both pilots and machines, but morale was still high. It was re-equipping and re-forming at Debden in Essex. In the first war it had been commanded by Major "Micky" Mannock, possibly the greatest fighter pilot in his day, and who was posthumously awarded the V.C. During its brief stay in France in 1939 and 1940 it destroyed 89 enemy aircraft.

So it was a proud moment for Peter Townsend when he arrived at Debden to assume command of this famous squadron. He entered into his new job with all his skill, determination, and thoroughness. Soon his untiring and brilliant leadership was to bring glory to the squadron and himself.

In the words of one of the pilots under his command: "Peter was one of the finest men I ever met. He was sensitive and shy and very sincere. With those people he knew well he was lively and amusing, a good conversationalist. He was a superb commanding officer because he was never harsh or rude, was balanced, and always interested in the welfare of everybody. He was liked by all ranks."

He was in the air every day and almost all day. He had firsthand experience in being outnumbered.

While on convoy patrol early one morning in July, he attacked a Dornier as it was shadowing a convoy. After firing at it the Dornier went into cloud and while searching for it, Peter heard a voice singing, "September in the Rain." "That means a rocket for Sergeant Hampshire (his No. 2) when I get back," he thought. A pilot who left his transmitter switched on jammed the rest of the squadron. But as Peter continued his search the voice in his earphone became louder. Then a moment later Peter came out into a large opening in the cloud to find himself in the midst of 30 Me.110 fighter-bombers. The voice in Peter's headphones was that of the leader of the German formation mixing his orders with snatches of song.

Peter signaled his base for reinforcements and then climbed above the Messerschmitts, biding his time to pounce. Peter had not read the tactics of Richthofen, the German ace of World War I, for nothing.

Twice Peter dived into the formation, which was circling in twos and threes, and barely escaped being shot down on each attack. Each time he got away with an enemy on his tail. Peter was a ruthless fighter but he calculated his risks. But there are moments when a fighter pilot must risk all. He always led his squadron into action brilliantly and courageously.

On July 10 he was shot down while patrolling over the North Sea soon after dawn. The weather was rather dirty when he spotted a Dornier reconnaissance aircraft. He came in to attack from astern and after an exchange of fire there was a loud explosion in Peter's cockpit. The Dornier had registered a hit with a high explosive shell. He called base, said he had been hit and was bailing out, giving his position as 20 miles east of the Suffolk coast. Although Dorniers at that time were not supposed to be equipped with cannon, Peter was certain that he had been hit by a cannon shell. By the time he baled out his Hurricane was out of control. As he floated down toward the sea he carefully took off his flying helmet and tied the ripcord to it, then dropped it in the water. After he had struggled to blow up his Mae West and disengaged himself from his parachute he noticed the helmet floating on the water a few yards away. He swam over and picked it up.

By now the minesweeper *Cap Finistere,* which fortunately for Peter was apparently off its course in a minefield, lowered a boat to pick him up. Thinking he was a German, the mate stood menacingly in the stern with an oar raised in his hand. Peter directed a flow of language at him which identified him beyond all possible doubt as an Englishman. Strong arms hauled him out of the icy water and within a few minutes a peg of rum had brought back some warmth to his shivering body. The trawler took him back to Harwich.

It was six o'clock when he was shot down. By afternoon he was back with his squadron and flying again. He had saved his parachute and his flying helmet. That night he telephoned his mother. She seemed more upset by his getting wet than by the narrow escape he had from being killed by the cannon shell.

August 18 was a red-letter day for Peter and his squadron. Leading 12 other Hurricanes, Peter met a formation of nearly 200 bombers and fighters. Although heavily outnumbered, the squadron immediately attacked, destroying 9 fighters and 1 bomber, probably destroying 4 others and damaging 6.

On this day the R.A.F. lost 27, the enemy 71.

Fighter Command was beginning to win the battle but it was not long before the German bombers and fighters were flying in much tighter formation. Fighter losses were heavy and the Command was drawing on slender reserves. If the battle went on too long the R.A.F. would be defeated.

From August 19 to 23 the Command was given mild respite because of poor weather.

Mass German daylight attacks were resumed on the 24th, but until September 6 there was only one a day. Destruction of the R.A.F. was still the object. On August 19 at a conference at his lodge, Goering said: "We have reached the decisive period of the air war against England. The vital task is to turn all means at our disposal to the defeat of the enemy air force. Our first aim is the destruction of the enemy's fighters. If they no longer take the air, we shall attack them on the ground, or force them into battle by directing bomber attacks against targets within range of our fighters. At the same time, on a growing scale, we must continue our activities against the ground organization of the enemy bomber units. Surprise attacks on the enemy aircraft industry must be made by day and night. Once the enemy air force has been annihilated, our attacks will be directed as ordered against other vital targets."

These were crucial days.

The full fury of the onslaught was now concentrated on the airfields of 11 Group in southeast England. On August 31 Croydon was bombed and again Hornchurch. And this was also a fateful day for Peter. The Battle of Britain had begun on August 12, and his squadron had been moved to Croydon —the front line. On this day, 85 were scrambled just as a formation of Me.110 fighter bombers with an escort of Me.109's were attacking from 8,000 feet.

The squadron was at lunch when Peter was told on the

telephone to get his pilots across to the Dispersal Point. They piled into their dilapidated cars (such was the haphazard organization because of lack of equipment) to drive at break-neck speed across the grass to their Hurricanes.

They took off as the bombs fell. At the head of his squadron Peter climbed at full throttle to engage the Me.110's but the escort of Me.109's, numbering about 20, dived to beat him off. Soon he was in a battle with them. In a sharp dogfight he attacked and hit two Me.109's. A third passed so close beneath him that he could see the pilot seated at the controls. He depressed the nose of his Hurricane and got his sights on the German fighter. As he fired he saw out of the corner of his eye the flash of a Me.110's guns ahead. The 110's bullets struck the Hurricane, tearing open the center fuel tank; the nosecap of a cannon shell smashed into Peter's foot. For some obscure reason the Hurricane did not catch fire, but Peter was soaked in gasoline and blood. He looked around for a place to land in the Kent hopfields, but below there was nothing but woods.

When his Hurricane was only 1,400 feet from the ground, he realized that a landing was hopeless and so, with little height to spare, he bailed out. As he floated down two maids stood in a garden, looking up at him open-mouthed.

Despite the ridiculous situation he was in, suspended a few hundred feet above the ground, he called down to them with his characteristic courtesy: "I say! Do you mind giving me a hand when I get down?" But he bumped on to the ground some way off, took off his shoe, looked at his wounded foot, and then heard a click behind him. He turned his head to find himself looking up the barrel of a rifle with which a zealous Home Guard had him covered. Peter was quick to establish his identity.

Peter had landed near Hawkhurst in Kent and was immediately taken to the cottage hospital. The policeman who retrieved his parachute arranged for it to be exhibited in aid of the local Spitfire Fund. It raised £5.

That night he was put into the back of a truck and after a bumpy journey arrived at Croydon General Hospital. In the operating theater the siren sounded as they started to give him the anaesthetic. The surgeon bent over him saying: "I'll save your toe if I can," and then started to work. But Peter was not yet unconscious and told the surgeon so. To prove his point, he spoke: "If you think I'm out, you're wrong. And if you don't believe me, I will tell you my right forefinger is crossed over my left thumb." The ether mask was clamped on again and he was out. When he awoke he was to learn that the big toe of his left foot had been amputated.

Soon he was harrying the doctors and nurses to let him out. Within three weeks he got his way and was back with his squadron, walking round with a bandaged foot and with the aid of a stick. The first thing he did was to take up a Hurricane. The Squadron Diary notes: "To the amazement of onlookers, he carried out aerobatics."

The Squadron had suffered such heavy casualties that it had been withdrawn to the Midlands and turned into a night-fighter squadron. Even with his injured foot Peter was flying operations every night. Flight Lieutenant Tim Moloney, the Squadron Adjutant, wrote in the Diary: "One of my major problems as an adjutant is to try to make the C.O. get sufficient sleep."

It was at this time that a young fighter pilot, Hugh "Cocky" Dundas, was first to meet Peter. Dundas wrote after the crisis of 1955:

"The first time I met Peter Townsend he was a squadron leader commanding a night-fighter squadron and I was a very young and junior pilot officer in a Spitfire squadron. I was not only a young and junior pilot officer that day; I was also a windy one. For I had just reported back after some very mild wounds and a very bad fright.

"Townsend was standing in the doorway of the officers' mess as I walked in with my new commanding officer. And, despite the gap between our respective positions, he spoke kindly and naturally with me.

"I noticed one of his feet was bandaged. After we had left him, my commanding officer told me that despite a serious wound in the foot he was flying operations every night.

"And at that point I developed an immediate hero-worship for Peter Townsend. I soon learned I wasn't the only one. You often read of an officer during the war who 'inspired others.' Well, Townsend was an excellent walking and flying example."

On the day that Peter had his toe amputated, it was announced in the London *Gazette* that he had been awarded a bar to his Distinguished Flying Cross.

On September 7, the German Air Force abandoned its offensive against Fighter Command sector stations and launched its all-out assault on London.

The pattern of the German invasion was now fixed: mass night raids on London, small bomber forces heavily escorted to attack airfields during the day. It was not until September 15 that the Germans forced their way through to London in daylight. They flew over a thousand sorties, losing 56 aircraft (Fighter Command claimed 187) against 26 British fighters. During the vital fortnight—September 7 to September 21—when the *Luftwaffe* was supposed to be delivering a knock-out blow, immediate aims completely failed. Morale in England was high, and Fighter Command was able to regain its strength.

In the fortnight before September 7 the enemy lost 378 aircraft and Fighter Command 277—5 British for every 7 of the enemy. In the fortnight from September 7 to September 21—when the main attack was on London—Fighter Command lost 144 aircraft as against 262 by the *Luftwaffe*—5 British machines for every 9 of the Germans.

Preparations for the invasion reached their peak during the third week of September. The Channel ports of France held more than a thousand barges and there were 600 waiting up the river at Antwerp. Britain's Bomber Command crippled 12 per cent of this fleet.

By September 23 German shipping in the Channel ports was beginning to disperse. A third of the barges had left. Destroyers were moving round to Brest. The German Air Force kept up its pressure on aircraft factories and there were big diversionary fighter sweeps. One of the enemy's last big days was September 27. Germany lost 45 aircraft trying to get through to London and the Bristol works at Filton. The R.A.F. losses were 28. And the *Luftwaffe* again suffered heavily on September 30—the last day of full-scale daylight operations. The balance was still in favor of the R.A.F.: 47 against 20.

The danger to Britain of invasion was over.

When the Germans opened their main night offensive in September, Fighter Command had only eight squadrons primarily allocated to a night role. None were equipped with aircraft specially designed for night interception.

Because the number of specialized night fighters was so small, Hurricane and Spitfire squadrons—or rather their more experienced members—had to do duty by night as well as by day. Peter's squadron was one which had to fulfill this unenviable role. There were only a handful of experienced pilots in each squadron trained for this, and good night-flying facilities were not available at their airfields. In bright moonlight the pilots had no great difficulty in taking off, navigating, and landing, but dark, cloudy, or foggy nights brought fearful hazards. Indeed it often proved impossible to send up fighters to intercept the German bombers which were having no navigational difficulties because they were flying and dropping their bombs by the aid of a radio beam.

By October, Peter, in spite of his injured foot, was night-flying operationally. He insisted on going up in all weather, which nearly cost him his life. On November 19, thick fog enveloped his air base after he had taken off. Visibility was nil. He felt his way down, flying blind to the flare-path—

there was no runway. When he sighted it he was not properly lined up with it, but it was too late to turn. The flare-path disappeared into the fog and Peter crash-landed. His Hurricane was badly damaged and Peter was slightly hurt. But he refused to rest. The next night he was up again.

One night Peter intercepted a Dornier in a cone of searchlights. It had its navigation lights on, a trick used by German pilots to infiltrate into the R.A.F. bomber stream returning from Germany. After hesitating for some minutes—Peter could hardly believe his eyes—he attacked it at close range, firing thirty rounds from each of his Hurricane's eight guns. The stream of bullets hit the Dornier's bomb bay, setting fire to the incendiaries. The Dornier started to go down on fire, then it pulled up in a steep climb. For a moment it was poised at the apex of the searchlight cone, three parachutes streamed out into the light, the bomber plunging in a last dive, its navigation lights extinguished as it hit the ground. Another bomber dropped a stick of bombs across the blazing wreck.

In February, 1941, 85 Squadron was re-equipped with Havoc aircraft, and in April moved to Hunsdon in Hertfordshire.

In May, while stationed there, Peter Townsend met Rosemary Pawle, the daughter of Brigadier Hanbury Pawle, who lived in the neighboring village of Widford.

One Sunday morning early in the summer, Peter approached the Brigadier and asked him for the hand of his daughter. It was not surprising that Brigadier Pawle readily gave his consent. Only a few days before, Peter, now a Wing Commander, was awarded the Distinguished Service Order, his third decoration for gallantry.

Despite wartime austerity, the white wedding in July, 1941, of Rosemary and Peter, with all the splendor of a peacetime ceremony, is still remembered by their friends. The Widford Church was too small to accommodate all the guests, so the ceremony was held in the thirteenth-century church in Much Hadham, two miles away. Tim Molony was Peter's best man.

There was a guard of honor formed by the men of 85 Squadron. A colleague recalls that during the champagne reception, Townsend cornered him and said anxiously: "I hope that the guard of honor has not meant that the servicing of the kites has suffered." From another man's lips, those words could have been a joke. To Peter they were not. Even on his wedding day, he could not forget his duty.

In those tense days of almost hourly fighting, many young pilots married. There was the urge for a few brief moments of stability. Death ended many of those marriages. Many broke down because they were too hasty. The latter pertained in the case of Rosemary and Peter. They were temperamentally unsuited to each other. And, yet, their marriage had all the necessary ingredients to make it a lifetime partnership—a typical English girl of the middle class marrying this British Saint-Exupéry, as a friend of mine so aptly described him.

For a time Rosemary lived with relatives at Widford in Hertfordshire. It was a time of separations and sorties, of much that is now forgotten save by those who shared the sharp sad glory of those days.

Then Peter started to do less flying. He relinquished, with great reluctance, his command of 85 Squadron, for a brief posting at 11 Group Headquarters at Uxbridge under Leigh-Mallory. He was a sad man at the night of his farewell party in the mess at Hunsdon. How he felt was recorded in the squadron diary the next morning before leaving the station. His message to the squadron said:

> "It has been an honour and a very great pleasure to have commanded 85 Squadron for the past year or so. While I do not wish to dwell too long on my great regret at leaving such a grand crowd, I can honestly say that I have never had a better year in my life. Keep on giving hell to the Hun."

His fellow pilots and all the ground crews, too, were sad to see him go. They knew they were losing a wonderful leader. As one fellow pilot said: "The moment before a vital decision he always seemed to hesitate. Once made, however, the decision was almost invariably the right one." Years later he appeared to hesitate before a vital decision, yet who will say it was not the right one?

Like most of the survivors of the Battle of Britain, Townsend's new posts meant promotion. By the end of 1941 he became the Station Commander at Drem in Scotland and four months later his first son, Giles—now at Eton—was born. In June of 1942 he commanded 605 Squadron but in October he went to the Staff College for four months. For six months of 1943 he was Station Commander at West Malling, and then in the autumn assumed command of No. 23 Initial Training Wing. By January, 1944, he was at the Instructors Flying Training School at Montrose in Scotland. Soon there was to be a step that would lead him into a new and unimagined world.

How strange it is that one thought, one action, can change a man's whole life.

That is what happened in February, 1944, to Peter Townsend.

The thought was not his. Nor was the action. They belonged to King George VI.

For a long time it had been the practice for the Services to nominate Equerries to wait on the King. They were good men. But for most of them the hot blood of battle had been diluted by the polish of the courtier.

The King decided he would have about him the men who had fought the ships, the aircraft, the armies of the enemy. He asked the Ministries to suggest names—the names of men more familiar with an operations room than a levee.

A dispatch box arrived from the Air Ministry. In it was a special secret file. In the file were the names of three officers and their records. And one read, Group Captain Peter

Wooldridge Townsend, D.S.O., D.F.C., and bar. As we have
seen, he had every right to have his name on that short list.
He was one of the very first of The Few.

Why the King should have studied this file of three names
and then said—as he did—"I want Townsend," no one will
know. It is true that he had met Townsend before, three
times, in fact. But those meetings were at investitures when
Townsend was one of many airmen.

It is also true that on these occasions they had chatted for
a brief moment. On the last occasion, when Peter went to
Buckingham Palace for his D.S.O., the King had said to him,
smiling: "What, you here again!" Perhaps the King had remembered the incident when he read Peter's record in that
file. But at the investitures Peter had had no opportunity to
show his quick wit—his almost feminine intuition.

But the King had chosen.

There arrived at Montrose a message from the Air Ministry asking Peter to report to the Chief of the Air Staff, now
Lord Portal. There was no indication of the purpose of this
surprise interview. When Peter saw Portal in his room at
King Charles Street, the Chief of the Air Staff told him of
the King's proposal and asked whether he would care to
take the post of Air Equerry. Peter accepted. But before taking up his appointment at Buckingham Palace, it was necessary for him to see the King in person. So far the King had
been considering the appointment on the basis of records and
recommendations from the Air Ministry.

It was a chill morning in February when Townsend, now
twenty-nine years old and as impeccable as hours of work by
his batman and tailor could make him, was saluted by the
sentry outside the gilded wrought-iron gates of the Palace
and then was shown into the King's study by a servant in blue
battle dress. It was a small sunny room decorated in the King's
favorite colors—light-green walls and dark-green carpet. The
interview lasted about half an hour. The King must have
asked many questions about Peter's life and Peter's family—

a family that for generations had served its country. So while the King was desirous of rewarding gallantry rather than of furthering the advantages of birth, Peter Townsend was really tailor-made in both respects. Also, from the standpoint of the Court, he was married to the right kind of woman. There is no doubt Peter made a good impression. A few days later the appointment was confirmed.

Peter was to become a courtier. He could live up to his school motto: Fear God, Honor the King.

In a month he had started work in the Palace.

If this story were fiction, it would be a picturesque touch in weaving the threads of a romance to have Peter meet Princess Margaret on the day he went to see the King for the first time. In fact, this is what really happened.

In those days the Princess lived with her elder sister, Elizabeth, at Windsor Castle. They came to London one day each week.

After Peter had left the King's room he was standing in the corridor outside the Equerries' room talking to one of the Household. Elizabeth and Margaret came along. Peter was introduced. To the thirteen-year-old Princess Margaret, Townsend was just one more of that army of Service officers who could be seen in the Palace at any time during those vital years of war.

And what did Townsend think of her?

The impression she created on everyone at that time was of a leggy excitable girl with a lot to say and very little time in which to say it. She chattered endlessly in a voice far louder than the usual murmur employed by the royal family. That first meeting came and went and had all the insignificance of two strangers meeting in a bus queue.

But from that moment Townsend was to be thrown into Margaret's company.

# The Princess

No family in the world is subject to so merciless, so unrelenting a stare of public scrutiny as the British royal family. And no member has had to suffer from this ordeal by publicity more than the Princess Margaret.

Most of what is written is awry, some of it scandalous, as if the dry shade of Wilkes had returned to the world to focus once again his vile distorting mirror on royalty.

Princess Margaret has borne all this as part of the burden of what Queen Victoria once described as "my much disliked position." We, in Britain, have come to take for granted this silent acceptance, by the royal family, of whatever personal afflictions public curiosity about their lives may bring.

One protection of royal persons lies in the very nature of the institution they embody, with its self-sufficient, almost mystical quality. Ordinary citizens who consider the matter may find in royal institutions a subtle and civilized constitutional device, the way of providing the State with a symbolism that satisfies the heart and mind of individuals, as well as the collective emotion of a nation; they may do no more than accept it as wonderful fantasy, a family life lived with nobility and grandeur to lighten the too-ordinary lives of others.

But there is another view, found more especially in those who, whether by their heredity or choice, give their lives to the immediate service of the Crown. For those at Court, the monarchy is an end in itself, something that has a life and a reality independent of its usefulness. Within this atmosphere preserved despite all the vicissitudes of history, members of the royal family may well feel of their official position as a clergyman feels about the change conferred on him by

52

ordination. They hold a rank that carries inalienable honors and inescapable duties; it inevitably makes their lives different from those of other people.

It is this high and serious quality of being set apart—by the grace of God, if you are thinking in terms of the royal title—that saves the Crown from corrosion by the nauseous publicity that is concentrated on it. And it is in this set-apartness rather than in the imaginary character and attributes that have been invented for her, that the Queen's sister can be understood.

Princess Margaret is a royal person and one who is perfectly conscious of what that state entails. That she is an attractive girl, gay, warmhearted, and alert, is incidental to the central purpose of her life. It is a formal life and a lonely one, hemmed in by Victorian conventions and disciplines that have almost vanished from English life elsewhere. Nevertheless, since she was in her teens, her circle of close friends has been rather more widely drawn than is usually customary in the royal family. It is only with them and her own relatives that she can feel quite relaxed and at ease in company. Elsewhere there is always the danger that remarks, no matter how lightly made, may be repeated and achieve false importance.

Princess Margaret's friends are an amiable and intelligent collection of young people; they are conventional in the sense of believing in moderation. But they are lively-minded and regard conversational dullness almost as a form of bad manners. Princess Margaret has never abandoned her pre-eminence, or, in the light of hindsight arising from her desire to marry Peter Townsend, has she wished to. The kind of gossip that often passes as wit does not amuse her. She discerns and dislikes what is bogus or pretentious with speed and possesses the wit to discourage it.

Most of Princess Margaret's private life is spent with her family. It happens to be true that the royal family, despite its extent, is congenial and united; furthermore, one can see that, in the special circumstances of royalty's set-apartness, family means more to them than it does possibly to people who possess greater social freedom. Certainly to Princess Margaret her family has always meant more than even her closest friends.

The Princess appreciates fully the pleasures of civilized conversation. Although she is not a Bohemian, she has outstanding musical and theatrical talents. Hence she became a fan and friend of Danny Kaye, not minding when he called her "honey" instead of "Ma'am." She is not an intellectual but is intellectually above the other members of the royal family. She is better educated and much quicker-witted than most people. To her mother she owes not only a most happy upbringing but a sense of humor that is as definite an asset in royalty as in any other kind of person.

With an instinctive desire to remain within the decent conventions, there goes a love of things that are British. Her religion is part of these feelings. She has studied it with an unusual care; her devotion to it became greater after her father's death. She practices it without ostentation. It is a very definite part of the serious side of her life.

And, yet, having said all this, one is conscious of the fact that in Princess Margaret's character is something of an enigma. As Annigoni, the noted Italian painter, said after finishing her portrait, "I painted her as a woman of mystery." It is possible that she is not completely understood by any member of her family or by her most intimate friends. Only in Peter Townsend did she find complete harmony of mind.

After her sister was safely settled in motherhood, Margaret became the most eligible party-goer in London. It was her chore to play to the hilt the ingénue lead in an elaborate comedy of manners. After the war British society, like an aged actress who has outlived her time, had fallen into neglect. But royalty's duty was the same as it had been: to set an example of good manners to every class. It was Princess Margaret's particular task to make it seem that everyone was having a ripping time at her parties. Newspapers wrote about every party the Princess went to, reporting her every dance, her every glance, her every girlish gesture. Shopgirls and Mayfair matrons read these stories and—just for a moment— austere England under a Socialist government seemed to be merrie England once again.

"Look into my eyes," Princess Margaret ordered a startled dancing partner. "I am looking into them, Ma'am," he stammered. "Well," said the Princess, "you're looking into the most beautiful eyes in England. The Duchess of Kent has the most beautiful nose. The Duchess of Windsor has the most beautiful chin. My mother, the Queen, the most beautiful complexion. And I have the most beautiful eyes. Surely," she added with an impish gleam in her eye, as her flustered partner groped for a suitable answer, "you believe what you read in the newspapers."

The Princess believed none of it. As a younger girl she may often have longed to call less cynical attention to her large, soft blue eyes and to kick up her heels in a freer fashion. As a princess she could only mock, strictly among her friends, and make the best of it. "After all," as one flag-waver remarked while welcoming her to Capri, "a king's daughter is still a king's daughter."

Princess Margaret was not born a king's daughter, but even the weather on the night of August 21, 1930, seemed to conspire with a sentimental people to give her birth a special glamor. A howling wind whistled around her grandparents' home, Glamis Castle, where Shakespeare's Macbeth had long since murdered sleep and Duncan. Lightning flashed and the rain beat down. The announcement of the first royal birth north of the Tweed since 1601—when Charles I was born at Dunfermline—was greeted by an ear-splitting squeal of bagpipes.

The Princess was born at nine twenty-two P.M. and weighed nine pounds. She was then fourth in line of succession—preceded by the Prince of Wales, her father, the Duke of York, and her sister Elizabeth.

The baby was christened Princess Margaret Rose of York, and for years was known as Margaret Rose. But the Princess disliked the name Rose and insisted on its being dropped.

Her grandfather, seagoing George V, was still king. Her great-grandfather had also been king and her great-great-grandmother was Queen Victoria, a stern little woman who wore nothing but black for forty years and was not easily amused. Neither was her consort, the Princess' great-great-grandfather, Prince Albert. On the other hand, the son of this dour couple, King Edward VII, the Princess' great-grandfather, was quite easily amused. In fact he was a scamp, in the endearing sense. But his eldest surviving son, King George V, the Princess' grandfather, was gruff and dignified and unamused. George V's eldest son, King Edward VIII, however, was easily amused and surrounded himself with amusing friends. He reminded the world of gay old Edward VII, just as his brother who succeeded him, George VI, reminded people of the dignified, duty-minded George V.

Thus it can be seen that there were two strong tendencies in the Princess' family, and the question was, which did she have? In retrospect the answer may seem to have been evident very early, although the signs were not so easy to read at the time.

When she was eleven months old and was being carried by her maternal grandmother, Lady Strathmore, she began to hum the "Merry Widow Waltz," an example of precocity so startling that Lady Strathmore nearly dropped her. When she was three a predisposition to look on the attractive side of dark matters was revealed. Her mother showed her a picture of a horrid-looking dragon, and the tiny girl clapped her hands and cooed, "Oh, Mummy! What a darling Loch Ness monster!"

On her third birthday, celebrated at Glamis Castle, Sir James Barrie came over to tea. Margaret was fascinated by a little toy table with two painted flower pots on it, the whole thing about the size of a thimble. The author of *Peter Pan* asked her: "Is that really yours?" To which came the immediate reply: "It is mine and yours."

So intrigued was Barrie by this answer that he incorporated it in the text of his play, *The Boy David*. And he acknowledged the source by promising the Princess a penny royalty for every time that particular line was spoken on the stage. Four years later as he lay dying, he sent his secretary, Lady Cynthia Asquith, with a bag of pennies to the Princess' London home. In return the famous dramatist received a receipt solemnly signed by Margaret and witnessed by her mother.

Margaret's father adored this child. Her favorite trick was to rush down the stairs from her nursery high up in 145 Piccadilly, peep round the dining room door, and time her arrival cunningly to coincide with the coffee stage. Squeezing against her father, she would be rewarded with a handful of special coffee crystals.

The King once said that his younger daughter could "persuade the pearl to come out of any oyster." As she grew up he could refuse her nothing.

If she was much loved by her father, so was she by her grandfather, King George V. She had an arrangement with him that at ten thirty every morning just before the changing of the guard she would wave her handkerchief out of the window in Piccadilly on the promise that he would do the same from his study in Buckingham Palace across the Green Park. After the King died she remarked: "Grandpa is in Heaven now. God must find him very useful."

Sometimes Margaret was the *enfante terrible*.

At four, finding the guests at a grownups' luncheon dull, she crawled under the table and tickled their feet. At six she showed the true mark of *joie de vivre*, an unrepentant spirit. After being sent to her room for some mischief, she was recalled with the honeyed words, "Come along, dear, you need not stay up here any longer. I'm sure you're good now, aren't you?" To this she answered, "No, I'm naughty still. And I'm going to go on being naughty."

And she did. Once she rowed to the middle of a pond and would not come back. Several times she frightened visitors by hiding in the palace draperies, jumping out and yelling, "Boo!" At twelve, despite the disapproval of her mother, the Queen, she not only dunked her biscuits in her tea but once said in public, grinning at a guest, "Mother doesn't like me to do it as she says it's not polite." At fourteen, when she was a Girl Guide and was rowing on the lake at Windsor Castle with a Guide mistress, she pulled the plug out of the bottom of the boat "to see what would happen." The usual thing happened. Since they were in shallow water, no real harm was done and she could safely enjoy the sight of the indignant Guide mistress wading in to the muddy shore, her skirts held high.

The same year, when as part of the Guide training in social graces she was told to write a letter answering an imaginary invitation, she composed the following: "Dear Lady Godiva, I am so thrilled with your invitation to your dance which sounds such fun. I shall do my very best to bring a partner, and would Lord Tulip do? Wasn't it wonderful fun at the meet on Monday? I did think Lady Adcock overdid it a bit, with that hat of hers at church, didn't you? Thank you again so much. Yours affectionately, Diaphenia."

During all these years there was at least the possibility that such behavior was the reflection of normal childish good spirits but that theory did not quite suffice when Princess Margaret reached her teens. Then the conclusion was reached that she enjoyed exceptionally good spirits and would be likely to go on doing so. On the female side she was undoubtedly the liveliest person her family had produced in several centuries, if not for all time.

If Uncle Edward had stayed on the throne, this would have been a matter of very small public interest. But when Margaret's father became King, he and his family became symbols.

Up to a point their symbolic functions were clear-cut. The King obviously symbolized a great deal—all things British, from the invincibility of the fleet to the custom of taking a long weekend. The Queen was his symbolic helpmate, representing the fundamentals of the British female character. The eldest child Elizabeth, as heir presumptive, ideally symbolized industry, devotion, and all the other wholesome attributes that make British children models of behavior. At a rally of the Mothers Union, Princess Elizabeth spoke out firmly against "growing self-indulgence, hardening materialism, and falling of moral standards" and urged young mothers not to be afraid of being thought "priggish."

There was, however, no specific job, symbolic or otherwise, for a younger child in the royal family. There might be advantages to the position; but there are drawbacks, too. For since the role lacks definition, everyone is entitled to an opinion as to how such a child should conduct herself.

Princess Margaret was five when her Uncle David became King Edward VIII and then a few months later before his Coronation in Westminster Abbey his reign was over. He abdicated so that he could marry twice-divorced Wallis Warfield Simpson, an American.

"Are they going to cut off his head?" Margaret asked her big sister expectantly when she heard the news. When she finally understood that her own father was to be the monarch, her interest gave way to broad impatience. "Oh, bother," said the Princess, "and I've only just learned to spell York."

Rapid changes on the throne made Margaret acutely aware of the monarchy, but they did nothing to change her status in her own family. She was the younger sister and could only become queen if Elizabeth died without an heir.

It would seem that Margaret never much liked her role. She did not dislike sister Lilibet—as she was known in the family—or envy her; she just never enjoyed second place. And perhaps Lilibet was always inclined to treat her little sister as an unpredictable child who must be watched.

The first really good look the world had of the sisters together was when they stood side by side at their father's Coronation, wearing identical robes of royal purple, trimmed with ermine. Reporters, cameramen, and radio commentators were fascinated at the sight of the six-year-old Margaret yawning, stretching, tapping her silver slippers, riffling through the pages of a prayer book, and tickling her sister, while eleven-year-old Elizabeth frowned and nudged her in lofty, outraged dignity. But the reporters would have been more fascinated had they been in Buckingham Palace and seen Princess Margaret kick up one of her worst tantrums. When she learned that Elizabeth's dress was to have a train and hers none, she raised such an uproar that the King himself called in the dressmaker and ordered trains for both girls' dresses.

She was so delighted with the train and the light-weight coronet that her father had had designed for her as well as her sister, that she would appear at teatime wearing it. "I'm wearing it to practice," she would explain, swaggering up and down the room, carrying a walking stick. "What are you pretending to be now," her mother would ask. "Why, can't you guess? I'm Johnnie Walker."

Margaret's bubbling imagination and great self-assurance were a buoy for Elizabeth's shy conscientiousness; dutiful Elizabeth was a steady rock for mercurial Margaret.

Nonetheless, the two sisters have always been fast friends.

Elizabeth was four when her sister was born and welcomed her by giving her her own favorite stuffed toy, an act of self-lessness that, so far as Elizabeth was concerned, was to set the tone for their entire relationship. The two little girls were close enough in age so that they could do many things together, and although they were different in temperament, they became very good friends and were fondly nicknamed "the inseparables." They shared a nursery, a governess named Marion (Crawfie) Crawford, a fifteen-foot-square playhouse given by the people of Wales, and a series of pets. In due course they collected stamps, went to the zoo, studied French, learned to ride bicycles and were otherwise enveloped in the social and educational paraphernalia of well-off children.

When Elizabeth at eleven became a Girl Guide, she insisted that Margaret be enlisted too. The younger sister was signed up as a Brownie, Leprechaun Six.

Whatever Elizabeth did, Margaret followed in her unpredictable way. When Elizabeth set out a neat garden of daffodils and tulips, Margaret planted rows of potatoes and pulled them all up to see how they were doing. While Elizabeth fondled her ponies and puppies, Margaret made pets of a salamander and a speckled toad. When Elizabeth won a certificate for life-saving, Margaret had her day: she heaved her sister's pet Corgi into the lake on the day of a Buckingham Palace garden party and dived in after him, triumphant and heroic in her best party dress.

In their studies together, Elizabeth applied herself with diligence while Margaret romped and pranked. But what Elizabeth achieved by perseverance, Margaret absorbed with much less show of effort. Elizabeth played the piano with skill and polish; Margaret switched from Handel to boogie-woogie when her teacher was out of hearing, but played even better. Music, like everything else, came easily to Margaret. Perhaps she did hum the "Merry Widow Waltz" at eleven months.

Although Elizabeth and Margaret were each other's best friend, there was always perhaps a tendency on the part of the younger sister to catch up with her elder sister. It never interfered with the affection between them. Nevertheless, Margaret always seemed to try to do everything better than her sister.

For example, after she became a Brownie, she plunged in with such pioneer zeal that she soon won a chestful of merit badges. She learned to swim and, at the age of eight, walked off with the Children's Challenge Cup at the Bath Club. As a pianist she became more than an accomplished amateur.

When painting lessons began Elizabeth was diligent and painstaking, while Margaret soon invented a character called the Pinkle-Ponkle, who lived in the air and liked to hover over towns. "If he were to come down," she explained, "he would find worm sandwiches and caterpillar jam."

But despite her own talents, no one was quicker than Margaret to recognize her sister's more solid qualities. Once, at the end of a stern lecture on behavior, she remarked philosophically to her mother: "Isn't it lucky that Lilibet's the elder?"

Margaret's only real concern during her childhood was to make sure that she was left out of nothing and never went unnoticed. When she felt neglected, she dropped salt for sugar in her sister's tea or substituted tapioca for bath salts in her bath. As Elizabeth grew older and began entertaining mixed company at Buckingham Palace or Windsor. Margaret cheerfully crashed the parties. It soon became evident that her glib tongue and her talents for imitating Bing Crosby or Burl Ives more than made up in the eyes of the young men for her gawky lack of years.

Encouraged by these early successes, Margaret developed these gate-crashing tactics to a fine art. In 1947, when Elizabeth was given the ceremonial Freedom of the City of London, Margaret showed up, too, via a side street, and her sister had to make a hasty appeal to the Lord Mayor to have her fitted in. The next year, when the rest of the family had gone off to the races at Ascot, leaving Margaret at home at Windsor Castle with firm instructions to stay there, she hitched a ride with a house guest and turned up in the Royal Enclosure, wearing the wrong clothes and a cheerful expression. She was seventeen; Elizabeth had not gone to the races until she was nineteen.

The truth is that by the time she was old enough to "come out" she had already been out, having "sneaked out," as one observer phrased it, several years before.

Margaret loves to see the people. At seventeen she lunched

for the first time in a public restaurant. She was the guest of her father's cousin, Queen Ena of Spain, who sent a message over the telephone to ask whether Margaret would rather lunch upstairs privately in her apartment or downstairs in Claridge's dining-room.

Back came the prompt reply: "Downstairs, please, so that I can see the people."

It was to see the people that she went to her old nursery in the front of Buckingham Palace and looked down on the crowds in the Mall cheering the bridal carriage bearing her sister and Philip to Waterloo station. Only a few minutes before Margaret had been at the gates of the Palace scattering rose petals over the newly married couple.

At ten, she shocked her sister by remarking that Buckingham Palace's footmen were a handsome lot. At fourteen she was caught red-handed sampling her father's champagne. At sixteen she was dabbing herself with Schiaparelli's "Shocking," and insisting on her right to wear lipstick. The Queen tried a tactful remonstrance. "Do you really think it's becoming?" she asked. Margaret answered by dragging her mother to see a movie short in which Elizabeth had been allowed to use lipstick, while she and the Queen went without it. "See, Mummy," said Margaret, "you and I look like suet dumplings!"

Sometimes the King tried to lay down the law but her parents found that the best way to keep their daughter in line was to give her her head.

So the young princess floated into the social swirl in Elizabeth's wake. At her sister's wedding she finally came into her own. There, for once, Margaret's taste and imagination were put to use by the family. When the problem of choosing dresses had to be faced, the Queen and her elder daughter, who in those days were not noted for their chic, were glad enough to listen to Margaret. "I do not desire to be a leader of fashion," said the Queen. "Well," replied the younger daughter, "I do."

When Elizabeth married, there were some who knew Margaret who predicted a crisis. They remembered how often she had said, when wanting something that her sister had been given or when trying to emulate her: "I want to be like Lilibet. I want to be like Lilibet." She always felt a little frustrated. And although she nearly always got her own way, particularly with her father, there were times when she did not.

Elizabeth had been given a car as a twenty-first birthday present. In time, Margaret wanted one, too. The King agreed to her request. But what kind of car did the younger sister want? Elizabeth had a sedate saloon. Margaret wanted a red sports model like that of her most faithful boy friend, Billy Wallace. But this was one time when the King refused to be swayed by all Margaret's charm and beguiling. The chosen car was a green saloon.

It was after her sister's marriage that the world's newspapers took aim on Margaret. They described her clothes, noticed her lively good looks and her beautiful blue eyes. She spent weekends at the country houses of titled persons, usually with a crowd of whimsically minded young people to keep her company, and passed so many late hours in London's nightclubs that one mass-circulation Sunday newspaper felt obliged to cluck its tongue at her with a deep black headline: "Princess Margaret's Week of Late Nights." She had so many escorts that she cost gossip columnists a good deal of energy trying to keep their names straight. They followed her to the nightclubs and peeped under tables to see with whom she might be holding hands. With wedding bells still ringing in the public's ears, every youthful Guards officer, every handsome young lord with whom Margaret danced twice, was publicized as a possible husband for the young princess.

In the days of her high-spirited teens, her behavior inevitably became a public issue. The pro-Margaret group, on a show of hands, would have won overwhelmingly. Her supporters were the great, then socialized, hard-working masses.

AIR MINISTRY

STANLEY DEVON, KEMSLEY

*Above.* 85 Squadron
—and Kim.
*Right.* 1947. South
African Tour.

1947. South African Tour.

To them the royal family has always been an outlet. Even during the years of wartime austerity, King George VI always rode on public occasions in a big Daimler saloon. He said it was part of the trappings of the Crown when it was suggested to him that a smaller car might be more suitable. In a word, the King was saying, if a docker cannot ride in a Daimler, the King could do so for all dockers. So, therefore, if the docker's daughter could not go to a formal ball or dance with the heir to a duke, the King's daughter could do so for all girls.

Even in those postwar days when newspapers were short of newsprint, the activities of the royal family were fully reported, with the result that Princess Margaret became, so to speak, the Joint National Debutante. As such she supplied romance, color, and girlish freshness to the then rather drab national scene. And if she added a touch of impudence and spice too, they said: "She's a natural sort of girl who likes a good time, the way all girls do. She'll have to settle down soon enough."

The anti-Margaret faction was found in widely separated areas among the unfashionable nonconformists. They grumbled about her late hours and dancing, or when she occasionally sipped a cocktail or smoked a cigarette. And there was a little grumbling among the rich, conservative High Anglicans, with their hereditary and vested interest in the Throne. They were disturbed by anything that might seem to detract from its dignity. As one of them recalls, flinching: "I was standing near the King and Queen at a Buckingham Palace garden party, a very sedate affair as you know, when there was the most awful noise a few yards away. It was Margaret, entertaining some friends with an imitation of Danny Kaye. Really!"

There were even more frowns when, just before her nineteenth birthday, she danced the can-can before three hundred guests at a private party at the American Embassy. This, of course, was the sort of incident that lent itself to newspaper distortion, particularly in the American press.

It was really a very decorous affair. Her close friend, Sharman Douglas, was giving a party at her father's residence in Prince's Gate. Sharman wanted it to be a fancy dress affair. Margaret consulted her mother—as she always does. The Queen thought it would be fun.

The midnight cabaret was kept a close secret. There was an expectant hush as the lights went down. Then, accompanied by Maurice Winnick's band playing the can-can music originally associated with the Paris *Folies Bergère,* eight pretty girls, their arms around each other's shoulders, appeared in a well-drilled line, kicking their legs in perfect time—but only to a very modest height and with an abundance of frou-frou of petticoats hiding their upper limbs. The audience, including Princess Elizabeth and Prince Philip who had gone to the party as an Upstairs Maid and a Waiter, went on applauding until a rather breathless encore was given. Margaret's great-grandfather, Edward VII, would have enjoyed it too.

But if Princess Margaret in those days was a gay girl, there was also a serious side to her character. She was fully conscious of her official responsibilities.

Even before her sister's wedding, Princess Margaret performed her first unassisted public duty, the launching of a liner at Belfast. She made a pretty little speech, and when a young shipworker came to present her with a bouquet of roses, she graciously selected one and tucked it in his overall's bib.

Margaret's first speech in public was made a few months after Townsend went to the Palace. She was not fourteen. It was made during a visit to the school named after her in Windsor. She was wearing a pink cotton dress with short white sleeves. She received purses from twenty-five of the pupils, past and present, in aid for a rebuilding fund. It was the first of many such ceremonies but this one to the Margaret

Rose School had considerable significance. It meant a milestone in her career as a public servant. She passed the test successfully, although it must have been something of an ordeal—with her mother looking on apprehensively to prompt her if necessary. She experienced not for the last time "first-night nerves." And she has confessed that she still gets them.

It might have been thought that her public performances in pantomime or, in later days at private parties mimicking a star, would make it easier for her to face an audience. But Princess Margaret draws a distinction between what she calls "make-believe" and the serious, dedicated side of her life. One is fun; the other *real*. For the latter she is always desperately anxious not to disappoint those who have probably waited many hours to see and hear her. But even if she is nervous there is no trace of it in her face. She appears self-possessed and puts at ease everyone around her.

If she had a speech to make she put much work into it. The draft of the Queen's secretary would be carefully edited by the Princess herself. And she rehearsed it beforehand, delivering it when the time came with the same irresistible sincerity that her mother and sister always showed.

It therefore distressed her when these speeches became the subject of criticism, it being argued that they were too conventional. "Surely it is the feeling behind them which matters," she protested. "Besides what do they expect me to do? Stand up and call out, 'Hiya, folks'?"

The Princess was right.

Not all the Princess' speeches, however, were a string of clichés. Six years after her first public speech at the Margaret Rose School, she spoke at the Camp Fire of the 13th World Conference of Girl Guides, held at Headlington Hall just outside Oxford. There were girls from the most distant corners of the globe. There was a moment which probably still lingered in their memories long after they got home.

Before the sing-song and the lighting of the Camp Fire,

the Princess spoke to the girls. As she reached the final paragraph, she paused and then, in a firm voice, said: "We shall be loyal to our ideals, which never change with time or custom; and we believe that by our example we shall help to establish true and lasting friendship among the nations of the world."

# The Airman and the Princess

"EQUERRY OF HONOR"—A PLEASING PHRASE. IT FITTED PETER Townsend like a glove. The change-over from the easy, well-ordered informality of R.A.F. life to work in the starchy, rarefied atmosphere of Buckingham Palace was surprisingly easy.

The life of a Court official is a very difficult one. It is a curious profession, usually followed by men and women with whom it is a family tradition. Most of the work is administrative, for it is their job to see that the details and the general workings of any royal function run smoothly. They must tactfully smooth the way when royalty visits an industrial town or attends a State function. They must help with speeches, carry bouquets, encourage the diffident, and discourage the overattentive, and they must stay discreetly in the background. But most of all it is a personal relationship and there must be a genuine liking between royalty and courtier.

At all this Peter Townsend was a success. From the first he was getting on well with the King, much better than many of the courtiers who had been in the Palace for years.

The King was already a sick man. He was highly strung and inclined to be nervously irritable when he was overtaxed. And during the war he found no rest.

Peter was well accustomed to that type of temperament. He had handled too many weary pilots who behaved exactly the same way. And the experience served him.

He is a vigorous organizer too. His first duties at the Palace were merely liaison with the Air Force. With that critical eye that had won him respect if not always enthusiasm at R.A.F. stations, he started to get things done, working from a small bleak office off the "business" corridor on the Constitution Hill side of the Palace.

The King soon appreciated the efficiency of his new Equerry. And he appreciated too the comfort and balm the airman could bring to a tired monarch. Once as Peter was called to the telephone, the King watched the slim figure in Air Force blue and said: "There is a man who can do things."

After the war, the King chose for him a Grace and Favor house in Windsor Great Park. He selected Adelaide Cottage, which sat behind a ten-foot-high privet hedge in a byway of the Park. It was the first home that Rosemary and Peter had ever had, but for all its royal association, life for them was rather wearing there. The cottage had been built for Queen Adelaide, wife of William IV, as a garden house and as a hideaway for pregnant ladies of the Court. The cottage overlooked beautiful gardens.

Electric cables were laid to the cottage from Windsor Castle. But the current was so weak that all the load it would carry at one time was a vacuum cleaner and a small electric heater. The inside of the cottage was gloomy, decorated with Victorian wallpaper, and heavy, ugly Victorian furniture.

I feel that there was some significance in the King's choosing a home for his Equerry so near to the Royal Lodge, Windsor, where he and the Queen and the young princesses preferred to spend their weekends. In a sense, the King had already taken Peter into the family. They were only walking distance across Windsor Great Park from each other.

Soon Peter was to get to know the royal sisters well. With the war still on, they were living at Windsor Castle. In 1940, after Dunkirk and when the country was threatened by invasion, the King had been urged to send Elizabeth and Margaret to the safety of Canada. There was a fear that when the invasion took place an attempt might be made by parachute troops to capture the royal family as hostages. But the King had refused to send his daughters away and in this he was backed up by the Queen. She said: "I wouldn't let them go without me and I cannot leave the King."

It was not an easy choice. Only a few weeks later, during a daylight raid, a bomb fell in the forecourt of the Palace. The King and the Queen were not in a shelter. The windows of the room in which they were sitting were shattered. An hour later they were visiting the East End of London and sympathizing with bombed-out victims. "Our home has been hit, too," said the Queen quietly.

In retrospect it is difficult to appreciate that Princess Margaret from the age of ten to fifteen was locked away in the Lancaster Tower at Windsor Castle. She left London a "little football"—her own description of herself—and returned a teenager to mingle with the crowds in the Mall on VE-Day—and probably knock off a few hats.

Already she was a rather sophisticated young woman, to some extent because of the environment of those five years. She was quite at ease with the young Guards officers who were on duty at the castle.

Occasionally these young officers were the guests of her sister Elizabeth at lunch. One, recalling the two young hostesses, said: "If you sat at Princess Margaret's end of the table the conversation never lapsed for a moment. You did not have to worry at all yourself. She was amazingly self-assured without being embarrassingly so. In fact, she was already a good companion."

At the weekends when the King and the Queen sought a few brief hours away from the war, they would arrange impromptu parties for their daughters. Once there was an invitation to Canadian airmen and during tea Princess Margaret was seen four times to be "dunking" her biscuit, until she finally received a look of remonstrance from her mother.

Then there were the informal suppers when the rugs were rolled back afterward and everyone would dance to the gramophone. Margaret would sip champagne when she thought her mother was not looking. Once Philip Mountbatten and David Milford Haven appeared on leave together. The two sisters danced happily, making a foursome for three nights running. It was the beginning of Elizabeth's romance.

And those were the days of the Christmas pantomimes at Windsor Castle. Peter saw his first at the Christmas of 1944, the last Christmas of the war. It was staged in the Waterloo Chamber of the Castle. The program said: OLD MOTHER RED RIDING BOOTS, devised by Princess Elizabeth, Princess Margaret, and Hubert Tannar.

Mr. Tannar was the headmaster of the Royal School at Windsor Park. When he died after the war the two princesses lost a dear friend. He was the producer of all their childhood pantomimes. Even the King was a contributor to the script, and was not too pleased if one of his jokes were cut. For instance, after a dress rehearsal Mr. Tannar received a telephone call from Margaret that her father had noticed that they had left out one of his jokes. "He thinks it is one of his best ones," added Margaret. "So please can we put it back again tonight?" It was put back.

These shows were enjoyed in the spirit of family charades and no one in the audience laughed more heartily than the King. One member of the cast had the poise of a professional. This was the principal girl named in the program as "The Honourable Lucinda Fairfax." There was an immediate quickening of interest when she came on the stage, and went up to the microphone. She waited quite self-assured until the applause subsided and she gave a little nod to the conductor of the orchestra. Then she sang "Sing a Song of Tomorrow, Today."

Princess Margaret was then only fourteen but if she had been any other person but a princess there would have been no speculation about her chosen career. Later she sang a duet with her sister, "Sur le Pont d'Avignon." Probably Peter Townsend, like the other members of the audience, found himself looking at the younger one. It was the same in the sketch that had as its focal point the queue for a No. 9

bus. Margaret's lines came across the footlights with all the insouciant gaiety of a soubrette destined to see her name in lights.

But two members in that cast would never experience the chance to make friends in a queue or experience the communion of such everyday incidents of life.

In February, 1945—the war now nearing to a close—the second son of Rosemary and Peter was born. Although Townsend had been an Equerry for only a year, the King as a mark of his esteem and possibly affection for his aide consented to be the boy's godfather. Peter Townsend acted as proxy for the King at the christening ceremony in St. George's Chapel, Windsor Castle, on Sunday, November 3, 1945. The boy was named Hugo with a second name of George after his illustrious godfather.

After the ceremony Princess Elizabeth and Princess Margaret went back to Adelaide Cottage for the christening tea. It was the first of many Sunday visits. Princess Elizabeth liked to chat with Rosemary, while Princess Margaret played with the children on the lawn, and Townsend, off duty, sat back in a deck chair. Sometimes the King and Queen arrived to collect their daughters, but more often Peter ran them home himself.

Margaret never went to Adelaide Cottage unless she was accompanied by Elizabeth or the Queen. Sometimes Rosemary drove Peter out to Windsor Park bridle path so that he could go riding with the sisters. But nobody can remember that Margaret ever showed she had even a schoolgirl crush on the handsome young Equerry.

At one tea party, young Giles stood behind a rhododendron bush and made faces at Margaret. Margaret stuck out her tongue right back. At a cocktail party Giles was permitted to stay up to say good night to the royal guests. His dressing gown was too disreputable to wear on such an occasion, so nannie put on a new pair of pajamas which she had recently made for him. Rosemary instructed the nannie: "For heaven's sake, button him up well, even if you use a safety pin. We don't want to embarrass Princess Margaret."

After they were married, Elizabeth and Philip, who had a weekend house at nearby Sunningdale, sometimes called at the cottage for tea or a drink.

How did the Duke and Townsend get along as individuals?

When he was first married the Duke was glad of Peter's company. He was a grown-up version of the boy next door. Peter by then was a confidant of the King. Edinburgh could have few close companions and it was very convenient to have someone in the Palace to chat and joke with.

When the Duke was completely preoccupied with his ambition to fly, he sought Townsend out and often they would be seen waving their arms and hands in aerobatic mimicry.

The fact remains that Townsend and the Duke were never close friends. Their temperaments are very different. As time went by their acquaintance was never warmed by any comradeship. Said a friend: "Philip is all man's man, and Peter isn't. Philip likes polo, although he's not a great horseman. He is a little contemptuous of Peter's gentleman jockeying."

Another truth is that Townsend was a palace servant. Philip was a member of the family.

But in fairness to Prince Philip, it must be stated here that he was *not* a vigorous opponent of his sister-in-law Margaret's marrying Townsend. He did not take an active part in the family discussions, although there is no doubt he discussed the problem privately with his wife, the Queen. Philip may have been apprehensive as to whether such a marriage would harm the Crown. Yet, he is very fond of his sister-in-law and must at all times wish for her happiness. In view of the manner in which he has publicly stood behind his former secretary, Commander Michael Parker, it must be assumed that Prince Philip accepts the modern view toward divorce and remarriage.

Except on the visits of the royal family to their cottage,

the Townsends entertained very little. Rosemary was, therefore, often alone with her two children and the servants.

Townsend normally had a two weeks' tour of duty, during which he worked in the daytime at Buckingham Palace in a high-ceilinged very old-fashioned room on the ground floor which he reached by way of the Privy Purse door in the forecourt used by all the Royal Household. The office had dark green walls, a marble grate with an open coal fire, an ancient mahogany desk, and long windows overlooking the gardens. At night he slept in a palace bedroom. If the Court was at Balmoral his room at nights was in one of the towers, a room still furnished with Queen Victoria's hideous tartan upholstery and bird's-eye maple, or at Sandringham, in a room decorated in white paint and chintz.

At the Palace Peter ate his meals in the Household dining room among the ladies-in-waiting and the private secretaries. It is a big circular room with a painted ceiling. Once it was a library and still has shelved alcoves to prove it.

During his tours of duty, Peter did not return home at all. Then he was given six weeks off, when he was home all the time. It was a routine not particularly conducive to married bliss. Rosemary was either a "palace widow" or a wife with a husband in constant attendance. The former meant days of boredom for Rosemary, and the latter situation was irksome to them both. These erratic hours put a strain on the marriage. Peter, an active man, got bored when he was not on duty. Time hung on his hands. To try and solve his problem, he went into the city and worked in Lloyds for an underwriter during his periods off duty from the Palace. But as time went on and his relationship with the King and his family became closer, Peter was inevitably away from home more and more. Then Rosemary complained to a friend: "Peter spends more time at his work than in his home." Slowly the marriage began to break up. It might have withstood the strain of Court life if Peter and Rosemary had been more temperamentally suited to each other.

Nevertheless, Peter's posting as an Equerry of Honor to the King turned out to be just what he wanted when peace came. He did not dwell in the past, as so many war heroes have done. His new life at the Court gave him intimate participation in that intangible, undefinable something, compounded of history, tradition, and the simple faith of millions, which give the British royal family a unique touch of magic. His strong sense of duty was now concentrated on service to the monarchy. His perfectionism and easy manner meant that his service was performed flawlessly and with no apparent effort.

Peter's real test as an Equerry came in the spring of 1947 when the royal family left England on the battleship *Vanguard* to start their long South African tour. It lasted three months and covered nearly 10,000 miles—nearly 5,000 miles by rail, 5,000 by air. From first to last Princess Margaret saw quite a good deal of Peter Townsend. He often rode with her and her sister.

As the tour progressed he began to notice that Margaret, thin and white-faced, was finding the tour a nerve-racking experience. Whenever he could, he helped her and encouraged her. Soon she began to find him more and more indispensable.

On the famous climb up the Matopo Hills to Rhodes's grave, Peter watched with amusement as Princess Elizabeth took off her low-heeled shoes and gave them to her mother to wear so that the Queen could walk more easily on the slippery granite.

Perhaps during this tour came the beginning of an easy, quite unselfconscious relationship between the Princess and Townsend, a relationship based on liking, trust, shared tastes and interests, admiration.

And during the South African tour, Peter endeared himself to the King. He made himself invaluable. Perhaps his happiest moment was when the King put his hand on his shoulder and said laughingly: "I don't know what we would do without you, Peter."

Peter was at Margaret's side again when, barely eighteen, in September the next year, she performed her first official act abroad—representing her father at the investiture of Queen Juliana of the Netherlands. Townsend sat two pews behind her in the great new church at Amsterdam. When, before the service began, she looked round nervously—like a child lost among so many grownups—his warm smile gave her confidence.

But there was one trip that Princess Margaret made when Townsend did not accompany her, although she might well have liked him to. That was her first—and last—Continental holiday. Perhaps it was a pity that Peter Townsend was not her aide on that trip. He was later to prove adept in handling newspapermen. His charm and finesse were sorely needed by the Princess during that sight-seeing journey.

After her eighteenth birthday, Princess Margaret, then very much under the influence of her girlhood friend, the vivacious Sharman Douglas, pleaded with her mother and father to let her take a trip on the Continent alone. The African tour had given her a taste for travel.

At the airport when she came home, she murmured politely: "I've had such a wonderful time."

It was nice of her to say so, but Princess Margaret's thirty-five day holiday had not really been so wonderful.

For more than a year the exuberant young Princess plunged enthusiastically into her plans when consent was given. But in almost no time, Whitehall, the Queen, the Embassies of Paris and Rome, and a host of palace aides were all involved.

By April, 1949, when the Princess stepped into one of the "planes of the King's Flight" in London to take off for Italy, her holiday had become a royal tour. Margaret showed no disappointment. And no surprise. "Isn't it a pity," she said to her father on their 1947 visit to South Africa, "that we have to travel with royalty."

Hounded by newspaper reporters, plagued by photographers, dogged by detectives, and ringed around by protocol,

prudence, and propriety, the little Princess had not had
what could be described as a rip-roaring time. Many an evening during her holiday, when the stars twinkled over Capri
or the lights of Montmartre beckoned, she had sat primly in
a hotel room chatting with her private secretary, Major
Thomas Harvey, and his wife.

When she did go to a Paris nightclub, she sat out all the
rumbas to avoid what might be interpreted as undignified
dancing for a princess. Even so a photograph of her that
night smoking a cigarette out of a long holder did not escape
ridicule. A woman wrote solemnly to a newspaper: "What an
example for the Sea Rangers of whom she is the Commo-
dore!"

A simple swim she took in the surf at a private estate on
the Bay of Naples filled the world's press with "bootleg"
pictures of royalty in a two-piece bathing suit. Editors snarled
at one another over problems of journalistic good taste.

On her third day in Paris, the Princess did what any
clothes-conscious eighteen-year-old girl would enjoy—she paid
a call on the fashionable dress salon of Jean Desses of whom
her fashionably dressed aunt, the Duchess of Kent, had
spoken favorably. Margaret had a lovely time but rival cou-
turiers were in a dither at the royal honor done to a com-
petitor. The next day the Princess soothed the tense situation somewhat by dropping in at Christian Dior's. And on
her last morning in Paris she visited the elegant establishment
of British-born Captain Molyneux in the Rue Royale. The
management purred: "We knew that she would come all the
time." But they were pretty apprehensive until she did.

Ambassadors, worthy dignitaries, and expatriate dowagers
all had to be mollified with the same nice sense of protocol,
and gay Princess Margaret, with a rather set smile on her
face, spent hours enduring polite platitudes, visiting the sick,
and lending her presence to a tedious round of formal re-
ceptions.

One day, as she was being shown France's historic baroque

palace of Versailles, the whole thing suddenly came into sharp focus for her. As she studied a massive oil painting showing a royal command performance of the Paris opera a century before, she spotted the look of infinite boredom on the faces of King Louis Philippe and his family. Without warning the Princess threw back her head and laughed loud and long.

As has been noted, the problem of publicity is something that plagues all members of the royal family. None, however, has suffered so much from intrusion into their privacy as Princess Margaret.

Before she became betrothed to Prince Philip, the Queen was the center of the speculative limelight. But with Princess Elizabeth it was easy to see where her heart lay. It was always so obvious that she had eyes for no one but Prince Philip. The sheltered life she had led made it impossible for her to pretend. And that was to cause her sorrow and teach Margaret a lesson.

One day Elizabeth went to a working-class area to attend a function. The crowd yelled, "Where's Philip? How's Philip?" They were loyal cries of affection but they pained and embarrassed Princess Elizabeth. Princess Margaret found her afterward in her private suite extremely distressed. She confided to her sister: "Nothing is your own, not even your love affair."

Margaret made a mental vow that when she fell in love she would keep it secret until the announcement of her betrothal. And she nearly succeeded.

Margaret thought a great deal about marriage. Once when discussing the marriage of two of her friends, a marriage of opposites, she said seriously: "I suppose I had better marry someone firm to keep me in order." Was she thinking of Peter Townsend? When necessary, he could be quite firm with Margaret.

As he walked along the red-carpeted corridors of Buckingham Palace, he would run into Margaret, trying out a new dress or costume, complete with accessories. Peter would stop and smile at this one-woman mannequin parade. His opinion would be sought.

Usually he approved of the new acquisition to the wardrobe but if he didn't he was frank. "It is not you," he would comment. The dress would never be seen again.

Margaret respected Peter's judgment because he knew about The Big Outside World. Of him she would ask: "Tell me, how is this done in The Big Outside World?" And Peter would tell her.

It was in these small beginnings that their friendship and affection grew. It was happy and uncomplicated. And there was their religion, or to put it more accurately, the spiritual side of their lives.

How did Princess Margaret manage to keep her affection for Peter Townsend secret for so long? As we have seen, she was determined to keep her true feelings from the glare of publicity. And yet she perhaps fostered some of the gossip about her alleged suitors.

But from the time she was seventeen, the rumors bubbled thick and fast. Some of the stories, like the raging *affaire* supposedly launched when King Michael of Rumania lent her a theater program, made her laugh.

Margaret's potential suitors, who, in fact, turned out to be nothing more than escorts to theaters, dinner parties, or nightclubs, had to be acceptable at Court. Their background, upbringing, and temperament had to be perfectly suited to fit into the cramped rhythm of Court life. For most men, brought up in freedom, such a life would not be merely irksome. It would be intolerable. That is why all the escorts have one by one married other girls. Margaret's life was fashioned so that she was unlikely to have an opportunity of meeting any man other than the scions of noble families, Guards officers, men trained from childhood to realize that the laws which govern the masters are often harsher than those they could inflict on any servant.

In their twenties, both Margaret and her sister were younger than their years. Their life was sheltered. They had not the normal worldly experience of girls of their own age. So Margaret's gay spirits went to those who could amuse her for the moment. Her most severe criticism of an escort was, "He's quite dull." And Margaret to this day abominates dullness.

Peter Townsend is never dull. And he loved the Princess partly because in his eyes she was never dull. In an off-guard moment he once said to me: "She is such a wonderful person to be with."

In the beginning there was certainly no thought of any deeper emotion than friendship between them. Margaret always called him "Peter"—and that was how he was addressed by the King and the Queen. But Townsend always addressed her as "Ma'am." If Margaret was the Princess, Townsend was still just as much the royal servant. He never forgot his role in those days.

Then, as now, Princess Margaret was too well trained not to realize what harm lack of dignity can do a royal house. She may still leave a gathering, as she has done, where an overly friendly guest addresses her as "Margaret." She calls by their Christian names only those of her childhood playmates with whom she has remained in touch and a few other young friends of several years' standing. But as far as the use of her own Christian name is concerned, the Princess observes the long-standing royal rule. In public—and this means when one other person is present—only royal relations call her "Margaret." She permits a few of her most intimate women friends to use her Christian name when they are alone together. At all other times they, like her nonroyal relatives, address her as "Ma'am."

All this sounds a little stuffy in these days when everything is being democratized. But Margaret does not allow herself to be completely hemmed in by traditional taboos. For instance, there was a guest of Sharman Douglas, an American girl, going round saying good-by and kissing her English friends in a slightly exuberant fashion, to be stopped only just in time from embracing the Princess, too. "Look out," called Sharman from the canasta table at the end of the room, "she'll be calling you 'Maggie' next." The Princess roared with laughter.

Princess Margaret has had her name linked with many alleged suitors.

Perhaps the favorite of all speculations was the Earl of Dalkeith, who had been a friend of Margaret's since the days when he was a lanky boy with red hair and freckles. She called him Johnnie and loved him as a childhood friend and "elder brother." While she was learning to drink pink champagne, Dalkeith was studying agricultural productivity. While she was out in nearly strapless evening dresses, he was tramping farms in shapeless tweeds.

At the time of the King's death he was frequently in the Princess' company. I think that both the King and the Queen always thought (at least hoped) that their daughter would marry Johnnie. There was ample evidence at the time that Dalkeith was looked upon with great favor by all the royal family.

It is not surprising that Dalkeith was regarded as a very eligible suitor. He is a Scot, heir to the Dukedom of Buccleuch, a godson of Queen Mary, and a nephew of the Duchess of Gloucester, his father's sister. His mother came from the Lascelles family. He did well in the war in the Navy, and became a good farmer in peacetime.

Dalkeith and the Princess had many interests in common. The Princess shares his passion for horses—riding is the one form of outdoor exercise she really enjoys. The only thing wrong with this alleged romance was that though fond of each other, they were *not* in love. Margaret was already in love with Peter Townsend.

In January, 1953—at the time Townsend's decree was being made absolute—Dalkeith married in St. Giles Cathedral,

Edinburgh, Jane McNeill, a well-known fashion model, whose father was a prosperous Hong Kong Queen's Counsel. Princess Margaret was present at the wedding. Because she showed a little emotion, some columnists hinted that it was a case of unrequited love. Another piece of nonsense. She was probably thinking: Could her own love have a happy ending?

No one spared a thought for the long-eyelashed, slim group captain, who, in fact, spent more time with the Princess than all these young escorts put together. If the list of escorts was large it was because Margaret could not have an evening alone with a young man. He must invite at least six other acceptable people. Nor could the party go to any cheap and pleasant restaurant.

So the blunt truth is that although she was a gay party-goer during her teens and early twenties, afterward she was often desperately lonely in the cavernous rooms of Buckingham Palace. It was then that the debonair Peter Townsend came prominently into the picture. And the King and the Queen encouraged him to "take care" of their daughter.

When they were on an official round of duties in Edinburgh, he was asked to keep Elizabeth and Margaret amused. He simply whisked them off to see a gangster film at the local cinema—in the 2s. 9d. seats.

While her deep affection for Peter steadily grew, the Princess did have a good many boy friends. But if they appeared to be young men in love with life—and they could all afford to be—and if they had to be capable of making her laugh, they had to have a serious side as well. For Margaret loves to argue theology, and philosophy too.

In those years one of the inner circle of her friends was Mark Bonham Carter, a publisher who was to become Liberal M.P. for Torrington. Mark, the son of Lady Violet Bonham Carter, married a divorced woman. He and his wife were one of the families who gave hospitality to Margaret and Peter during their to-marry-or-not-to-marry crisis.

There are only two bachelors left among the Princess'

friends—Mr. Billy Wallace—now known as "Old Faithful"—
and that brilliant Anglican priest, the Reverend Simon
Phipps, cousin of Joyce Grenfell, the actress, whose grandmother was an Astor.

It has been said that Billy Wallace has long been under
Margaret's spell and might even still marry her. Nothing, of
course, can be ruled out. The Princess' choice is narrowing
and she is restricted in her opportunities to meet eligible
men.

This brings us to Simon Phipps, now a Chaplain to Trin-
ity College, Cambridge. Margaret and the Queen Mother
often lunch with him in his chintz-decorated chambers in
Great Court, Cambridge. They are very happy in his company.

Simon Phipps is the son of a Gentleman Usher to the
Queen, served in the Coldstream Guards before he was ordained, became a major, won the Military Cross. His first
priesthood was in Huddersfield. He likes to do "off-beat"
things. In a long vacation he took a nonunion job at £7 a
week as a carpenter. In a sermon afterward he startled his
congregation with "Both the Church and the trades unions
are high and dry and out of touch."

He occasionally takes Margaret to a theater and he himself
has a flair for writing revue sketches. This is a sample:

> "Can anyone think of an original sin?
> Just tell me someone where to begin.
> I have tried them all singly, mixed up in a medley.
> But those seven sins are so absolutely deadly,
> There must be another, I just can't wait
> Until I've discovered Number Eight."

This kind of thing helps to endear him to Margaret and so
does his deep theological knowledge, which they discuss for
hours. It is within my knowledge that he exerted more influence on the Princess in reaching her decision not to marry

Peter Townsend than did the Archbishop of Canterbury, Dr. Fisher.

In August, 1950, the extent of the favor Peter Townsend enjoyed at the Court was shown when he was appointed Deputy Master of the Household. He served directly under Sir Piers Legh, Master of the Household, in the domestic administration of all the royal homes.

When Princess Margaret celebrated her twenty-first birthday at Balmoral in the following August, Peter was on duty as Equerry-in-Waiting. By now he was a firm favorite with her. On the afternoon of her birthday the King, accompanied by the Duke of Edinburgh, Billy Wallace, and the Earl of Dalkeith, had gone off shooting on the moors.

The Queen with Princess Elizabeth and Princess Margaret, and three ladies-in-waiting, had a picnic on the heathered hills on Staunyarroch, above Crathie. One man was left with the royal ladies: Peter Townsend.

The party was surprised by a press photographer. When the Queen and the Princesses spotted the photographer's camera poking through a taxi window, they called: "Look, photographers!" The ladies-in-waiting looked—but Peter turned his back on the camera.

Later in the week the photographer came across Princess Margaret and Group Captain Townsend riding in a meadow adjoining the Balmoral estate. He took a photograph but was disappointed because the man in the picture was Townsend, an Equerry, and not Billy Wallace, an eligible bachelor.

Townsend was always very happy at Balmoral. He enjoyed the family atmosphere that reminded him of the halcyon days he had spent as a boy on holidays in Somerset with his mother. He looked forward to joining the royal family for dinner in the cream-walled, red-carpeted castle dining room with its shining candelabra-decorated table and with its pipers in full Highland dress.

If Peter enjoyed the peace of the moors, grouse shooting did not appeal to him. Stalking deer, however, did. He liked the arduous day-long tramp across the Highlands in search of the quarry, which might not be found until nearly sunset. It is a sport requiring great skill and perseverance. And you have to be a good shot, which Peter is. Perhaps stalking reminds him of his days as a fighter pilot during the war. War in the air and stalking are somewhat akin.

When the King and his friends left for the moors in the morning for a day's shooting, Townsend stayed behind to attend to his duties and then, sometimes, went riding with Princess Margaret. She does not like killing. Just before noon, they would join the shooting brakes that took the ladies in the house party up on to the grouse moors around the castle for a picnic lunch with the men.

Once, arriving at the butts on a blustery afternoon, Townsend joined Margaret and a party of her friends in one of them. The Duke of Edinburgh, a persevering shot, was a few butts away. He is not keen on having women near him when he is shooting, unless, like his wife, they are good shots. Their general talk and, frequently, their disinterest in what is going on sometimes upsets him. On this occasion, Townsend, Margaret, and a friend were being noisy. After a few moments the Duke turned toward them and shouted: "For goodness sake stop that awful racket!"

Usually Townsend went to Balmoral for his "holiday" tour of duty and when it was over he nearly always stayed on at the invitation of the King and the Queen.

A friend gave this description of Peter's position in the Balmoral family circle.

"We motored over for dinner at seven thirty. At least three footmen came out of the front door to open the doors of the motor cars. Peter and another member of the Court were waiting at the entrance. He showed us into where everybody else was in the drawing room, having a drink.

"There were eighteen or twenty guests to be introduced. On the table was a guest plan. Peter was responsible for working it out with the King and the Queen. Peter was also responsible for seeing that everybody knew where to sit at dinner.

"Timing is an enormously important element in royal life. Everything has to be arranged on the dot. Peter got us down a long corridor and into the dining room. The King sat in the middle of the table and the Queen opposite. The conversation followed the King. Peter sat in the least important place.

"After dinner Peter showed people into the cinema. There was no seating arrangement, but he hovered around until everybody was seated before he sat down himself.

"The film show over, the guests and neighbors left, but Princess Margaret and the intimate clique began playing guessing games, charades, or canasta. The royal family adore games.

"Peter was always on hand to make a fourth. If they decided to dance to the radiogram, he was always hovering, always at hand. He was not mad about dancing. But he had a quick eye for a wallflower and would rush up and ask her to dance."

By the end of the Forties the Townsend marriage had broken down.

And by this time the King had had one lumbar operation to improve the circulation of the blood in his legs and relieve the intense pain. Later he had to have a lung removed. Townsend was often his close companion.

It was not generally known outside the royal family circle that the King was always a short-tempered man. And, as noted earlier, when he began ailing, he became testy. Some friends say that the Queen Mother's rather vague, not-to-be-flustered, and at all times charming manner, is a defense she built up through the years to cope with an irascible husband.

Nobody, apart, of course, from the Queen, could soothe the King and make him relax better or ease his suffering more than Princess Margaret and Peter.

The Christmas of 1951 was spent by the King and his family, as always, at Sandringham. And it was to be the last. That year the King was too ill to make his Christmas broadcast "live" but he had spent many weary hours recording it word by word, sentence by sentence, so that the world should not know how difficult it had become for him to talk. The King was a dying man.

Peter was at Sandringham, too. Although deeply distressed by the King's health, his duties made this a pleasant period for Peter. The King was planning a health-restoring trip to South Africa, and to Peter had been entrusted the difficult task of going to South Africa immediately after Christmas to choose a house in which the King, the Queen, and Princess Margaret could stay. This was the kind of job that suited Peter's temperament. He is never more happy than when organizing a tour. And this was to be a very special tour in which everything was to be left to him. Over Christmas there was much talk about the plans, the voyage aboard the *Vanguard*—the ship that had taken them all to South Africa in 1947—and about the best place for the King to stay.

As it was the South African winter, it was agreed that Natal would provide the most desirable climate for the King. It was already arranged that the *Vanguard* should reach Cape Town toward the end of March and arrive in Durban three days later.

Peter left by air for South Africa the weekend of January 14. On his arrival he said to newspapermen: "I saw the King during the weekend. He is looking very well. The Queen and Princess Margaret are excited at the thought of visiting South Africa again."

He inspected the Prime Minister's official residence, Botha House, in Natal Province. Dr. Malan, an ardent nationalist and republican, had become a warm admirer of the King after a long talk with King George during the South African tour. So he personally offered Botha House as a temporary home for the King's convalescence. Peter's mission completed, he flew back to England and on to Sandringham to report to the King.

On the morning of February 6, 1952, the royal valet, James MacDonald, went to his master's room and found King George VI dead. He had died in his sleep during the night.

On the previous evening, Princess Margaret had played the piano and sung to him, while the King worked on a jigsaw puzzle. Once she had left the piano and moved across the room to help him. It was the last thing they did together.

"Life seemed to stand still after Papa died," Margaret wrote to a friend. "What a long time before I shall see him again."

Margaret wept a great deal. For many nights she had to take sedatives in order to sleep. She showed more signs of distress than any other member of her family.

Never a big eater and always fussy about her food, she almost stopped eating altogether. Only her breakfast remained unchanged: coffee and orange juice. She lost weight. For weeks, with her face free of make-up, she looked pale, almost transparent.

Each day after having breakfast alone in her suite, she would walk around the palace gardens with her mother's two Corgies and her own Sealyham, Johnnie. She would try and coax her mother out into the fresh air.

In her grief Margaret turned to the church. When a member of the royal family has a troubled soul and wants to ask questions about life, there are apt to be few in his limited circle of friends with whom he can talk. Outside this circle, the only source of moral and intellectual solace, accompanied by the necessary discretion, is the church.

After the death of her father and before the coronation of her sister, Margaret attended postconfirmation classes at St. Paul's Vicarage in Knightsbridge, as well as a series of eleven Lenten lectures on God and the eternal life delivered by the Bishop of Kensington.

Because her every move is watched, this development of her religious life led a Pakistani newspaper to print a baseless rumor that she was planning to enter a convent.

Princess Margaret still remains religious in a genuine sense. She often goes to church twice daily—slipping off by herself to Communion at eight o'clock and returning with her mother to the morning service.

Like many men who have faced death a hundred times, Townsend, too, is a deeply religious man. He is a keen student of the Bible and often quotes it to his friends and his enemies, to admonish them. His knowledge and belief, revealed in talks with Princess Margaret, gave her strength and comfort. He became almost her sole companion, the two spending evenings together when the Queen Mother had retired to her apartments to be alone with her grief.

Apart from her natural sorrow, her father's death significantly affected Margaret's life in another way. After her sister married she had been living at Buckingham Palace, the darling of the nation and the apple of her parents' eye, while Elizabeth and Philip lived in Clarence House, secondary quarters. The accession of Elizabeth led to Margaret's withdrawal to Clarence House. Her role was changed. She became the unmarried sister living with her mother in the second-best home. One Sunday newspaper which printed seventy column inches about her in a period of three months before her father died, had only seventeen in three months a year later. She had ceased to be a breakfast-table topic. Her sad remark: "Nothing seems the same without papa," was true in more than one sense.

Townsend, too, was white-faced and miserable. The King had been a very close friend. And one of his last memories of the King was a joke that he made during the preparations for the holiday in South Africa.

The last time that the royal family had been away the Queen and the Princesses had all gotten far more sunburned than they liked. Whenever Peter met the King to talk about the new trip, the King would laugh and say: "Don't forget the sunburn lotion."

With the death of the King, the world suddenly stopped

discussing a future husband for Princess Margaret. The windows of Buckingham Palace looked blankly on to a London stirring into spring.

Princess Elizabeth, now Queen, was occupied with picking up the reins of monarchy. Again Margaret was alone. Court mourning barred her from the light-hearted friends who might have consoled and cheered her, but in her grief, Margaret probably preferred near solitude anyway. Townsend was always near at hand. Before it had been the King who shared his daughter's problems and listened to her chatter. Now Townsend became the only recipient, though the Reverend Simon Phipps, whom Margaret met through Peter, was able to bring her great spiritual comfort, too.

Townsend gave her now all the fuss and attention which her nature needed. Without affectionate interest Princess Margaret—warmhearted and highly strung—is distressed. Life becomes empty, meaningless.

Therefore, the Queen Mother was grateful for the tireless energy of Townsend during the period after the King's death, for his care of her daughter, for his great efficiency. In any case he had been a great favorite of the Queen Mother from the moment he went to the Palace.

On the King's death he was immediately appointed Extra Equerry to the new Queen but it was not surprising to Court circles when it was learned that he was to become Comptroller of the Queen Mother's new establishment at Clarence House.

By the summer, the Queen Mother and Princess Margaret were preparing to move from Buckingham Palace into their new home across the Mall.

Townsend became the key figure in this change-over. He was the liaison between the decorators and the royal occupants-to-be. He talked with the Queen Mother and the Princess for hours about color schemes and furniture. Margaret wanted a large airy suite with pink as the motif.

When the move took place in August, Townsend left his

office on the business corridor of the palace and moved into a small house in the mews behind Clarence House. He set up a bare apartment for himself on the first floor.

Already everyone in the country was discussing the Coronation, set for the following year. It was, therefore, not surprising that on December 20, 1952—only five days before Christmas—a paragraph in the newspapers slipped by almost unnoticed. It read:

"Group Captain Peter Wooldridge Townsend, an Extra Equerry in Waiting to the Queen, was granted a decree nisi in the Divorce Court yesterday on the grounds of misconduct by his wife, Cecil Rosemary.

"Mr. John Adolphus de Laszlo, an export merchant, was cited as corespondent. Group Captain Townsend was awarded costs and given custody of the two children."

Townsend took a long time in deciding to bring this action against his wife, although he had not been living with her for many months before the King died. Rosemary and the two children left Adelaide Cottage toward the end of 1951. But it remained Peter's home. In fact, he lived there until the spring of 1953. He did not wish the Court to be embarrassed. But the King understood and was sympathetic and so was the Queen Mother. Her feelings toward him were no different when the decree was granted. She confirmed Peter in his new role as Comptroller of her household.

In February, 1953, two months after the divorce, Rosemary married de Laszlo, the son of a well-known portrait painter.

Now Townsend was with the Queen Mother and Princess Margaret almost constantly. He often had lunch or dined with them. In effect, Clarence House was now his home.

And everyone at the Court was too busy with the Coronation to notice the development in the relationship between Townsend and Margaret. Margaret's name had been linked romantically with no less than thirty-one eligible young men, but scarcely anyone outside the royal circle, and not even all the members of the family, were aware that the couple were in love. Perhaps it was because they had been seen together for so many years. It may have been because he was first a married man and then a divorced man, and therefore considered ineligible. But except for that it was perfectly logical. It is almost traditional that high-born young English ladies fall head over heels with their father's equerries or aides.

If the Queen Mother was aware of her daughter's feelings, then at first she refused to admit it. It is almost certain that the King knew of Margaret's love for Townsend long before he died. There is the story that one night Margaret and Townsend returned from a late party to the Palace. At the foot of the stairs, Margaret asked Peter to pick her up and carry her upstairs. Townsend demurred, at which point Margaret said, "That is a command, Peter." The command was obeyed, but halfway upstairs one of her shoes fell off and as they were laughing the King appeared on the landing in his dressing gown. Townsend put Margaret down. Frank explanations followed. But the King was not really deceived.

It may be asked: Why did the King permit his daughter to go on spending so much time in company with his Equerry? The answer must be found in the fact that the King was then a very sick man. He could only bear around him, his wife, Margaret, and Townsend.

So indirectly the King was partly responsible for his younger daughter's falling in love with his Equerry. When did they realize they were in love? It is possible, and I think probable, that the Princess was in love with Peter Townsend long before he fell in love with her. I do not think that even after his own marriage had broken down—and this was long before divorce proceedings—Peter ever saw himself as a suitor for the Princess' hand.

But it is not difficult to understand why the Princess fell in love with this good-looking, gallant airman. As we have seen, Princess Margaret from her childhood did not always enjoy playing second lead to her sister. She revealed this in her life in a hundred ways. Was she, therefore, a little envious of her sister when she married the glamorous young naval officer, Prince Philip?

If one takes a close look at Margaret's possible suitors of her teens and early twenties, there was no one who quite measured up to Philip. But Townsend did. He was good looking, possessed the qualities of almost eternal youth, had fought in the war like a knight errant, and was three times decorated for gallantry in the face of the enemy. Peter is a man whom women like. Why should Princess Margaret not have fallen under the spell of his charm?

For a long while it had been known that the Princess was more patient, more attentive, and more interested in the company of men several years older than herself.

The knowledge that they were in love with each other came no doubt in 1952, during the Court's summer holiday at Balmoral. These long summer days were perhaps the happiest they have ever been permitted to have together. In the years before Elizabeth's marriage, Townsend had often accompanied the Princesses on their early morning rides. As the years went by estate workers noticed how Margaret tended to drop back and ride alongside Townsend while Princess Elizabeth rode ahead. After Elizabeth married, Peter and Margaret rode alone.

Today there is very little left at Balmoral to remind people of Peter Townsend except an old coat. It was for a while being worn by one of the kitchen boys.

But there is another story which the romantic Deeside Scots people love to tell.

One of the favorite horse rides of Margaret and Peter was to the top of a hill in sight of Balmoral. At the summit, while the horses rested, they sat together on the heather and gazed around at the hills of lovely Deeside, each one capped by a stone cairn erected by Queen Victoria in commemoration of marriages and other family events. Peter and Margaret often talked of these cairns and the romantic association pleased them both.

The villagers say that in the summer of 1952 they were sitting on this hill when Margaret, perhaps almost as a dare, placed the first stone for a new cairn. Peter, to please her, followed suit. Then it became a habit, a game. Each day the first one to reach the top of the hill placed another stone on the pile. And so today, on a heather-covered hill where there is nothing to remind a man or woman of the complications of the world, there is a rough cairn, three feet high, built by a princess and an airman.

That was in the summer of 1952. But as I have said, the Princess had been in love with Peter Townsend long before that.

The rain came down. The low clouds sagged dismally over a Hertfordshire airfield. It was a June day in 1951.

Princess Margaret was then twenty years old and very lovely. She stood by the side of a man in an open-necked shirt and baggy, unpressed corduroy trousers. The man was Peter Townsend. Together they looked bleakly at the Old Hawker Hart biplane—G-AMBR. Nearby, officials were deciding the weather was unfit to stage the King's Cup Air Race.

The crowds, however, were not looking at the parked aircraft. Their eyes were on the Princess and the pilot. It was the third year the couple had entered the competition—and yet the Princess had never shown any other sign of being interested in aviation.

"Why," asked the experts of air racing, "should the Princess be here at all?" They were not to know that she was more fascinated by her pilot than her plane. As far as the public was concerned, Townsend was a man in the shadows. The world may have been busy picking a husband for the Princess. But the public was not to know that the Princess was playing a game of her own. She knew whom she wished to marry. Meanwhile she was busy matchmaking with her exclusive circle of friends.

If their love had been growing over a long period, it was not until April, 1953, that Peter Townsend and Princess

Margaret decided to marry. It has been suggested that a crisis was created by reports appearing in American newspapers early that year. That is not strictly accurate. The royal family was not taken by surprise by press reports.

As soon as the couple decided that they wished to marry—and they were fully aware of all the complications—they took independent action.

Peter Townsend went to the Queen's secretary, Sir Alan Lascelles, and told him that he and Princess Margaret wished to be betrothed. Townsend expressed his willingness to leave the Court if his continued presence was an embarrassment to the Queen and the Queen Mother.

Simultaneously, Princess Margaret asked her sister, the Queen, for permission to marry the Group Captain. And she told her mother that she was in love with Peter.

Perhaps if the Queen, the other members of the royal family, and Court officials had not been preoccupied with preparations for the Coronation, a different course of action might have been taken. As it was, the Queen tried to side-step the issue temporarily.

The Queen was very sympathetic toward her sister. She had not forgotten how her father, King George VI, had hesitated for more than a year before giving his consent to her marriage to Prince Philip. During those months of anguish and apprehension, Margaret had always reassured her sister that all would come right in the end.

The Queen consulted Sir Alan Lascelles. His advice was clear-cut: The Queen as Governor of the Church of England could not give her consent under the provisions of the Royal Marriages Act of 1772 to Princess Margaret's marrying a *divorced* man. He urged that Townsend leave the Court and be given an appointment abroad.

The Queen rejected this advice. She felt that this would be treating her sister too harshly, and that it would be better to let matters stand as they were. Any precipitate action might bring a spate of publicity, which could only do harm.

*Right.* Balmoral. *Left to right.* Rory Mc-Ewen, Simon Phipps, Billy Wallace, Peter Townsend.
*Below.* 1953. North Ireland. Last official duty as Equerry.

Day of reunion,
October, 1955.

The Queen counseled her sister to have patience. Perhaps she felt that Margaret's love for Townsend was only a passing infatuation. However, she had to tell Margaret that whatever her final decision, it was impossible for the Queen to give consent to the marriage. And that meant that the Princess had to wait more than two years until she was twenty-five and free from requiring the monarch's approval of her marriage.

Meanwhile, Sir Alan Lascelles had taken the initiative in consulting Sir Winston Churchill, then Prime Minister. And Sir Winston, in turn, asked his Attorney-General, Sir Lionel Heald, to prepare a full report on the Constitutional position, and informally to seek the reaction of Commonwealth countries to the marriage.

Sir Winston shared Sir Alan Lascelles' view that it would be disastrous to the monarchy at the beginning of a new reign for the Princess to marry Townsend—a divorced man (although the innocent party) from an obscure family and with little or no money. This might be regarded as the Victorian approach. He, too, thought it would be better if Townsend left the Court, especially as he was now part of the household of the Princess' mother, and so spending more time in Clarence House than out of it.

But neither Sir Alan nor Sir Winston could ignore the wishes of the Queen, so they did not press for Townsend's removal from the Court.

Thus matters were left until the Coronation. But Princess Margaret, always a strong-willed girl, had made it perfectly clear to her sister, to her mother, and the other members of the royal family, that she had no intention of renouncing her love for Townsend and that a way had to be found through the legal tangles for her to marry him.

Townsend throughout acted perfectly correctly. He placed the Princess' happiness first and in this he has never wavered to this day. If separation between him and the Princess had been the wish of the Queen, he would have accepted without demur. But separation was not asked.

The bombshell burst the day after the Coronation. But for Princess Margaret's brief indiscretion in the Great Hall of the Annex to Westminster Abbey it might have been possible to keep out of the British press the romance between her and the Group Captain. In the Great Hall were not only British newspapermen but also American reporters. The latter were perhaps more interested in the love affair of the Princess than in the Coronation. Stories had been appearing in the American press for many months.

No one can criticize the Princess' spontaneous act on Coronation Day. It was an hour of great emotion just after the crowning ceremony and what could have been more natural than for her to reveal to the world her feelings toward Townsend? But that small gesture was sufficient to open the floodgates of publicity. The next day the New York press was full of the story. And a week later, a British mass circulation Sunday newspaper, *The People,* broke the news to the British public. This was the story:

### THE PEOPLE SPEAKS OUT

"It is high time for the British public to be made aware of the fact that scandalous rumours about Princess Margaret are racing around the world. Newspapers in both Europe and America are openly asserting that the Princess is in love with a divorced man and that she wishes to marry him.

"Every newspaper which has printed the story names the man as Group Captain Peter Townsend, Equerry to the Queen and formerly Deputy Master of the Household. He is 38.

"The story is of course utterly untrue. It is quite unthinkable that a Royal princess, third in line of succession to Throne, should even contemplate a marriage with a man who has been through the divorce courts.

"Group Captain Townsend was the innocent party in the divorce proceedings. It was he who secured a decree last year against his wife, Rosemary, on the grounds of adultery. She has since married John de Laszlo, son of the famous portrait painter.

"But his innocence cannot alter the fact that a marriage between Princess Margaret and himself would fly in the face of Royal and Christian tradition.

"It is quite certain, therefore, that relations between the Princess and the Queen's Equerry have not gone further than is normal and customary between a member of the Royal Family and a devoted servant.

"The fact remains, however, that newspapers outside Britain have for weeks printed reports of their forthcoming marriage *without meeting any official denial*.

"As a result, the scandalous statements have been reproduced and enlarged upon. And it is to put a stop to them that 'The People' now places the facts before the public.

"When the Government and the Palace officials are faced with a popular clamour in Britain for a denial, it will be forthcoming.

"It is surely intolerable that immediately after the Coronation, one of the most widely circulated newspapers in the United States, the 'New York Journal-American,' should print entirely unrefuted statements like these:—

> Margaret is undergoing a strong emotional experience. The two who are being mentioned in her life and in whose company she is often seen are Group Captain Townsend and Mark Bonham Carter.
> Although in public Bonham Carter appears to have the lead, behind the scenes the Group Captain is considered the strong favorite.

> *The Queen Mother seems to favor Peter Townsend.*

"Another American newspaper, the 'New York Daily News,' goes so far as to say that the Archbishop of Canterbury and the Queen 'are having private conversations on the subject. Elizabeth knows fully well about her kid sister's romance and is said to be sympathetically inclined.'

"In France, these shocking rumours were given their biggest fillip last night by a long article in the well-known Paris weekly, 'Samedi Soir.'

"Pointing out that Group Captain Townsend, besides having divorced his wife, is the father of two boys, this news-

paper even declares that Princess Margaret is ready to renounce her Royal Titles and privileges in order to marry
him.

"All this is false. Handsome, charming, honourable though
Townsend is, and though he is a Battle of Britain hero who
wears the ribbons of both the D.S.O. and the D.F.C., it is
far beyond the realm of possibility that he should marry
Princess Margaret.

"Nevertheless, the rumours and statements about 'romance' and 'marriage' will continue to spread if they go
unrefuted.

"By withholding a denial the authorities are guilty of
letting the good name of the Royal Family, of a distinguished
Court servant and of Britain itself be dragged through the
mire.

"We believe that the British public, now informed of what
the world is saying, will be behind 'The People' in demand-
ing an end of this official silence.

"LET THE TRUTH BE MADE KNOWN. THAT IS
THE WAY TO STOP SCANDALOUS RUMOURS."

I have quoted this article in full for two reasons: First, it
broke the news to the British public of the romance between
Princess Margaret and Peter Townsend; second, the printing
of this story was not entirely a matter of journalistic enter-
prise.

So long as the Queen refused to agree to the "banishment"
of Peter Townsend from the Court, the Court officials, with
their vested interest in the Crown, felt themselves powerless
to stop the romance from maturing. If Princess Margaret and
the Group Captain were to continue to see each other daily a
marriage was probably inevitable. And these officials were
against the marriage.

So far the British press had refrained from speculating
about the affair, as it had done during the romance of King
Edward VIII and Mrs. Simpson. Perhaps Sir Alan Lascelles
and Commander Richard Colville, the Queen's Press Secretary, felt that it was in their interests to have the story broken

in London. Even if they did not inspire the article (virtually an editorial) they were quick to put it to their own use.

On Monday morning of June 15, 1953—the day after the article appeared in *The People*—Sir Alan and Commander Colville went to the Queen with a copy of the newspaper. They said it was now impossible to stop the British press from discussing the affair between Princess Margaret and Group Captain Townsend. Only one course of action was open: Townsend *must* leave his post as Comptroller of the Queen Mother's Household and he *must* be given a post abroad.

Still the Queen hesitated.

This time Sir Alan had an all-powerful weapon: publicity adverse to the Crown.

That afternoon he went to 10 Downing Street to seek the aid of the Prime Minister, Sir Winston Churchill. He asked Sir Winston to use his influence with the Queen to secure Townsend's "exile" from London. Sir Winston agreed to raise the matter at his regular weekly audience with the Queen the next day.

At this meeting Sir Winston was in a stronger position than when the matter had been discussed a few months previously. Sir Winston had had informal talks with all the members of his Cabinet and he had also discussed the problem with the Prime Ministers of the Commonwealth, who were in London for the Coronation and for a Commonwealth Conference.

This is how Sir Winston summarized the situation. The Cabinet was unanimously against the marriage. If such a marriage were proposed after Princess Margaret was twenty-five and free from the control of the Queen, Parliament would be unlikely to agree to it unless the Princess renounced her right of succession and that of any heirs of the marriage and also gave up her income under the Civil List. All this would require a special act of Parliament and under the provisions of the Statute of Westminster, similar Acts of Parliament would have to be passed by the Parliaments of Canada, Australia, New Zealand, and South Africa.

The Attorney-General in preparing his memorandum had consulted the Commonwealth Premiers and found that some, particularly the Canadian, were apprehensive about altering the royal line of succession. Canada argued that the line had been altered when King Edward VIII abdicated to marry Mrs. Simpson, and that to alter it again within twenty-five years could only prove harmful to the British monarchial system. If it was made easy for a member of the royal family to contract out of the succession, it might prove just as easy to make a King or Queen of some person who was not in line. If the hereditary principle were accepted it must *not* be tampered with.

The Queen was impressed by these arguments and promised to give immediate consideration to Townsend's leaving London. But first she must discuss the situation with Princess Margaret. She did not wish to hurt her feelings.

Some months earlier, the Queen had sought the advice of the Archbishop of Canterbury, Dr. Fisher. He said that Christian marriage was indissoluble and that the Canon Law of the Church of England did not permit the remarriage of divorced persons while the wife or husband of the former marriage was still alive. The Queen, therefore, as the temporal Governor of the Church could not sanction her sister's marriage to Group Captain Townsend.

After talking with the Prime Minister, the Queen again discussed the problem with the Archbishop. And then she talked with Princess Margaret. Townsend at this stage was barely consulted.

As the result of the discussions between the Queen and her sister the situation was speedily crystallized. Princess Margaret made it quite clear, both to the Queen and her mother, that she was deeply in love with Group Captain Townsend and that she had every intention of marrying him. She accepted the position that her sister, the Queen, could not give her consent to the marriage. She was willing to wait—and so was Townsend—until she reached the age of twenty-five. She also accepted the proposal that Townsend should be given a post abroad. But she would not agree to an appointment which could be interpreted as banishment.

However, a period of separation was insisted upon and accepted by the couple. It was strictly adhered to. This requirement—again rather Victorian in approach to the problem—came from Churchill to the Queen. It did not have the effect of ending the romance for all time, as was no doubt the hope of some. Separation only strengthened the love that the couple had for each other.

At the time of these discussions between the Queen and Princess Margaret, preparations were being made for the Queen Mother and the Princess to visit Southern Rhodesia in July for the centenary celebration of the birth of Cecil Rhodes. Townsend was to accompany them. It was now agreed that he should not go and that his place should be taken by Lord Plunket.

This change, of course, was a great disappointment to the Princess. She had been looking forward immensely to the tour. One concession, however, was made to her. Townsend should not take up his post abroad—at that moment it had not been fixed—until she returned from Africa.

The problem of finding a post for Townsend overseas was handled by the Prime Minister personally. He gave instructions to the Air Minister, Lord de Lisle, that there must be no delay. Townsend was given a choice of three posts: one at Far East Headquarters in Singapore, a second in Johannesburg, and a third as Air Attaché in Brussels.

The last was the obvious choice. Townsend had two young sons in England. It was natural for him to wish to have them during their school holidays. A distant posting would make that virtually impossible. Also, as no restriction had been placed on Peter's communicating with Margaret by letter or telephone, Brussels offered every advantage.

And it must be stated here that the Queen and the Queen Mother did not object to an arrangement whereby the Princess and Peter could communicate with each other. Nor did the Queen or the Queen Mother raise objections to Margaret's insistence that Townsend should from time to time come to London to see her after the first year. And this he did. Elaborate cloak-and-dagger arrangements were made for his trips and to my own knowledge he came to London and visited the Princess in Clarence House at least a dozen times. Further, they were able to talk to each other frequently on the telephone.

Arrangements for Townsend's departure from London moved along much more speedily than either the Princess or Peter had planned or envisaged.

Margaret and her mother left London Airport on June 29. Peter was not there to see the Princess off. They made their farewells in privacy at Clarence House. They would still have a few more days together in London when she returned from Rhodesia before Peter took up his new appointment.

The next day Townsend flew to Northern Ireland with Queen Elizabeth and Prince Philip. And the following day while he sat with the Queen and the Prince at a civic luncheon in Belfast, Buckingham Palace announced that Group Captain Townsend had been posted to the British Embassy in Brussels as Air Attaché.

The idea that Townsend accompany the Queen and the Duke of Edinburgh to Northern Ireland came from the Queen herself, although it did not meet with the full approval of Court officials. But the Queen felt it was a public gesture of faith in her sister and in the airman who had been a member of the Royal Household for nine years.

When the royal party arrived back at London Airport from Belfast, Townsend was the last to leave the aircraft. The Queen was already standing by the door of her Rolls Royce when he came down the gangway. She turned and walked a

considerable distance across the tarmac to smile warmly and
shake his hand. She seemed to be saying with her eyes: "Be
patient, everything will come out all right."

Thus ended Peter Townsend's life at the Court.

It was her mother who broke the news to Princess Margaret. Outside their hotel at Umtali in Southern Rhodesia,
the African sun shone hotly. Inside the Royal suite there was
a distressed Princess: Group Captain Townsend had already
left London for Brussels.

What a harsh task it must have been for the Queen Mother
to have sought that one moment away from the pomp and
pageantry so that she could turn to her daughter and tell her
that Peter would not be waiting for her when she returned
home. But the moment was found. And in the space it took
to tell, the gay Princess lost her smile.

A promise had been broken—a promise that Townsend
would not leave until she returned from Africa. The actual
parting had come with all the sudden bright-sharp thoroughness of a guillotine. Margaret had not expected that.

In London the announcement had already been made.

Townsend had not broken faith. He had protested without avail against his leaving before the Princess returned to
London. No doubt those who made this arrangement thought
they were acting in the best interests of the Crown. It was a
cruel move and only served to alienate the Princess from
those who opposed her wishes. It strengthened her determination to marry Townsend—whatever the obstacles.

Margaret had not objected to the stipulation that she and
Peter Townsend be parted for a time so that they could look
at their situation with an objectivity brought about by separation. She knew that Elizabeth and Philip had been separated for months before their betrothal was approved by
King George.

But what upset Margaret in Umtali was the fact that there
was to be no good-by at all. When the news was told to her

by her mother, Margaret flew alone to Government House in Salisbury, Southern Rhodesia. She immediately telephoned her sister and protested. And she phoned Peter Townsend.

The Queen cannot be held entirely responsible for what happened. It was the formidable palace organization which moves fast and surely when the occasion warrants. So speedily were the arrangements made that Sir Christopher Warner, the British Ambassador in Brussels, was not even sent a courtesy message hoping that he did not object to the appointment. As we have noted, Sir Christopher was at the time a guest of the Belgian Government in the Congo, and received the news of Townsend's arrival in Brussels from a Leopoldville newspaper. When he returned to Brussels, this very experienced diplomat, a stickler for the protocol, protested in no uncertain manner the discourtesy that had been shown to him by the Foreign Office. The Foreign Office explained and was apologetic. But it was an embarrassing situation for Townsend. Nevertheless, he was fortunate in having as his superior, Sir Christopher, a man of such deep understanding of the world. The Ambassador made it clear to Peter from the start that if he ever felt he needed advice, it was always available. From time to time Sir Christopher's help proved invaluable.

In Salisbury an official statement was issued. It declared that Princess Margaret had a heavy cold. A doctor—a heart specialist—was called in and gave her sedatives.

There was surprise at the circumstances in which she was brought back to Salisbury. The twelve-mile route to Kentucky Airport was closed to the public. Traffic was delayed. All available police—off-duty men, as well—were brought in to close the road.

The Governor, Sir John Kennedy, sent an aide to Kentucky airfield to wait for the Princess. *It was all an elaborate feint.* Princess Margaret's plane landed at Belvedere Airport on the other side of the city. Local editors were asked to play down her cold. The crew of the Southern Rhodesian aircraft was forbidden to say anything about what happened on the flight.

The royal tour progressed. But the Queen Mother traveled alone. For forty-eight hours Princess Margaret stayed in bed. On the day they were reunited the Princess first went to Communion. It was a subdued but officially "quite well" Princess who hugged her mother and kissed her. They were both misty-eyed.

The rest of the royal program was carried out. It was a great ordeal for Margaret. Those who lined the African streets were as well acquainted as the rest of the world with the strident rumors of the affection between the Princess and the Group Captain.

Transcending their joy at the royal visit was their fascination with the Townsend story. The crowds stared at the Princess long and curiously. And what did they see? Certainly not the gay vivacious Margaret London knew so well. The Princess' obvious sadness caused the rumors to flourish more strongly than ever before.

When the tour was over and the Princess returned to England, the same curiosity, the same anxious stares were to meet her.

And if Margaret's white face and small smile were anything to go by, then the evidence showed strongly her grief over the sudden departure of Townsend.

At Clarence House there was no material evidence that he had ever been there—just a couple of old jackets which he had given to a footman for his off-duty wear.

Britons were touched and some were shocked by the news: their favorite Princess was in love. This time the news had the ring of authenticity. It was not the story of a glittering princess who had found her Prince Charming in the fairyland of Mayfair, but a girl whose increasingly sober face in the news pictures seemed to reflect a deeply troubled heart. Family loyalty, religious responsibility, the duty of royalty—

all seemed warring with romantic impulse in the pretty Princess' heart.

It was understandable that the gossip writers had overlooked the slim, personable Group Captain, even though his pictures had been appearing alongside Margaret's for years. Probing the secrets of the Princess' heart was a continuous job for the world's newspapermen in London but they forgot the Holmesian precept that the most easily overlooked clue is often the most obvious one.

The first reaction of the British press, as exemplified in the article in *The People* was that such a romance was "quite unthinkable." But soon it was a subject of controversy.

On Friday, July 10, the independent Socialist weekly *Tribune* published an editorial written by its editor, Michael Foot, in these terms:

> "*Tribune* believes that Princess Margaret should be allowed to make up her own mind whom she wants to marry. Most other people, we imagine, would agree with that simple proposition. But the British Cabinet does *NOT* agree.
>
> "According to our information, the Cabinet was asked for its advice on whether the Princess should be allowed to marry Group Captain Peter Townsend. The Cabinet said 'No.'
>
> "The objection is based on the fact that Peter Townsend had been involved in a divorce case. That, in view of the Church, is a reason for preventing him from marrying the Princess, even though Peter Townsend was an innocent party in the divorce action. When the Queen referred the issue to the Cabinet, the Cabinet agreed with the Church.
>
> "This intolerable piece of interference with a girl's private life is all part of the absurd myth about the Royal Family which has been so sedulously built up by interested parties in recent years. It recalls the hypocritical role played by the Church at the time of the Duke of Windsor's Abdication.
>
> "Edward was loudly acclaimed as 'the best of Kings' until he expressed the firm desire to marry the woman he loved.

Baldwin and the Archbishops did not approve his choice. So they pushed him off the Throne.

"Now Margaret wanted to follow a course which did not exactly fit the prim conventions laid down by the Church. The Church was critical of what she wanted to do—just as leading Churchmen criticised Anthony Eden when he married again having divorced his wife. And the cowardly Cabinet has supported the views of the Church.

"The incident is not made any more savoury by our knowledge that three members of the present Cabinet have themselves been involved in divorce cases.

"The laws of England say that a man, whether he has divorced his wife or been divorced himself, is fully entitled to marry again. In some respects, those divorce laws are still too harsh. But no self-appointed busybody has the right to make them still harsher. If those laws are good they are good enough for the Royal Family."

This article was an embarrassment to both the Cabinet and the Palace. To the Cabinet, because three senior ministers had been involved in divorce actions. They were: Sir Anthony Eden, who at the time was gravely ill, Sir Walter Monckton, and Mr. Peter Thornycroft. Mr. Thornycroft had been divorced by his wife and had married again. Both Sir Anthony and Sir Walter had remarried. Another member of the Government, Mr. Ernest Marples, Parliamentary Secretary to the Ministry of Housing, had also divorced his wife.

The *Tribune* article sparked off a spate of newspaper controversy.

On the same day, no doubt acting under the influence of official guidance, the Political Correspondent of the Press Association, wrote:

"I understand that the Cabinet has not at any time considered the possible marriage of Princess Margaret and Group Captain Peter Townsend who, until his recent transfer to Brussels as air attaché at the British Embassy, was one of the Royal Equerries in London. The matter is understood never to have been referred to the Cabinet for advice.

"In the event of the Queen wishing for any guidance as
to Ministerial opinion, the most likely course would be for
her to consult simply the Prime Minister or whichever senior
minister was acting for him. There is, however, no reason to
think that this has been done."

In a sense this denial was accurate. The Cabinet had never
been *formally* asked by the Prime Minister to give an opinion
on the issue. The situation had not arisen when Government
action was necessary. In fact, it never did arise, even during
the crisis two years later. But, of course, the problem was
discussed *informally* among the Cabinet and by the Commonwealth Premiers, Mr. St. Laurent for Canada, Mr. Menzies
for Australia, Mr. Holland for New Zealand, and Dr. Malan
for South Africa.

And the article in the *Tribune* was quite accurate in substance—the British Cabinet ministers were against the marriage, just as Baldwin's Cabinet was against the marriage of
King Edward and Mrs. Simpson. True, the issues in the
proposed Margaret-Townsend alliance were not as vital to
the prestige of the Crown as in the case of the King and Mrs.
Simpson. But a marriage between the Princess and Townsend
was viewed with disfavor because it was against the principles
of the Established Church, of which the Queen is the head.
Such a marriage could only reflect to the discredit of the
monarchy.

The Liberal newspaper, *News-Chronicle,* in a leading
article commenting on the *Tribune* article, stated:

". . . There is an unhappy prospect that this private and
human problem may take on the aspect of a partisan political issue. That would be a thoroughly undesirable development. . . .

"If the young princess wishes to marry Group Captain
Townsend are there any just and proper reasons for denying
her wish?

"There could be no thought that in making the marriage

she would be falling short of the moral standards the nation and the Commonwealth desire to preserve.

"If the marriage were forbidden the sacrifice which the Princess would be required to make would be one which an enlightened age could not in good conscience demand.

"It seems highly probable that the vast majority of loyal millions in Britain and elsewhere in the Commonwealth would feel in their hearts that an official ban on such a marriage would be deeply wrong. . . ."

By the Sunday morning Lord Beaverbrook's *Sunday Express*—an old champion of the Edward-Simpson romance—was proclaiming: IF THEY WANT TO MARRY, WHY SHOULDN'T THEY?

But the austere Church of England newspaper shook a stern finger. Princess Margaret, it warned, "is a dutiful churchwoman who knows what strong views leaders of the Church hold in this matter. . . . The thought of the religious principle concerned might cause to some the very deepest suffering."

By the next day the powerful, independent *Manchester Guardian* had entered the fray. It wrote:

". . . What would be the general feeling in Britain and the Dominions if the Princess should wish to marry someone whose only apparent handicap was that he had been the innocent party in a divorce? One imagines that the answer would hardly be in doubt. A section of the Church of England and the Roman Catholic Church might make a protest as they did when Mr. Eden married last year. But to most people it would seem that this is a private matter in which so long as the law of the land is observed we should not interfere.

"It is true that the Princess is not exactly an ordinary person. She is close to the succession to the Throne and she performs public duties. But the succession is already pretty well assured without her; and there are other solutions if a Regency should unhappily become necessary. And the mass of ordinary simple people would not care two hoots when she came to lay a foundation stone or open a town hall whether her husband had been married before or not. Even if the question is entirely academic and speculation idle there is no harm in getting these things straight. It would be sad if, should such a case ever present itself, we had the unedifying spectacle of a battle of the texts and a division of the churches. This would not redound to the credit of organised religion. But might not more lasting harm be done to religion and to the popular attitude towards it, if the people felt that a princess had been made a sacrifice to theological prescriptions about which even clerical authorities differ?"

The *Manchester Guardian* suggested that the problem of the Regency could easily be solved. In fact, when the *Manchester Guardian* made this statement, the Queen, the Queen's ministers, and the Prime Ministers of the Commonwealth had already discussed during the Coronation period the question of the Regency and had reached a decision.

By the end of the last week in July, the Prime Minister, Sir Winston Churchill, was gravely ill. It became known that he had suffered a stroke (contraction of the blood vessels in the brain) and that it had been followed by a relapse.

So it fell to Britain's acting Prime Minister, the dry, donnish Mr. Richard (Rab, to his friends) Butler, to tell the House of Commons that the Government proposed to change the law which designated Princess Margaret as Regent should her sister, the Queen, die before Prince Charles reached the age of eighteen.

The 1937 Regency Act, said Mr. Butler, should be altered. The plan was to make the Queen's husband, the Duke of Edinburgh, Regent. The Queen felt it proper that Prince Charles's father, not his twenty-two-year-old Aunt Margaret, should train the boy for responsibilities of the Throne and shoulder those responsibilities as Regent if need be.

The Government, it seemed, was deliberately relieving the

Princess of one great obstacle to her marrying a commoner, the dashing Peter Townsend. But Butler made it clear in the House that the Regency change had been in the wind for more than a year. The question of freeing Princess Margaret to marry Group Captain Townsend—a matter requiring the approval of the Queen—had nothing to do with it. "Such a matter . . . has never come before the Cabinet," said Butler, "and I think I am voicing the opinion of all members when I say that . . . deplorable speculation and gossip should be brought to an end."

But Mr. Butler hoped in vain. The gossip grew even louder. It has assumed "the shape of scandal" protested the stately, pompous *Times*. And it was obvious that the gossip was going to continue for a very long while.

There were immediate rumblings against the de-emphasis of Princess Margaret and a stir because of the new emphasis on Prince Philip.

Lord Beaverbrook's *Daily Express* and the independent liberal *Manchester Guardian*—which find few issues to agree upon—both agreed that the Regency should be kept "in the line of succession" rather than pass to one not in the line. In a word, Princess Margaret should have the Regency if her sister died before Prince Charles, the heir, was eighteen.

The *Manchester Guardian* wrote:

"There will be many who feel that the custom embodied in the 1937 Act should not lightly be set aside. It seems to be more in the spirit of the traditions of the British Monarchy that the Regency should be kept in the line of succession rather than pass to one [Prince Philip] who is not. The need for change is not obvious, although a minor change to include the Queen Mother among the Counsel of State, who act during the Sovereign's absence from the country, will obviously be welcomed."

Charles Wintour, one of Beaverbrook's political writers, under a headline in the *Sunday Express*, "Now Don't Meddle" wrote:

"The position that would occur today if the need for a Regency should ever arise is not widely known. In 1937 a Regency Act was passed by a National Government with a Conservative Prime Minister, with the object of making a permanent settlement for such an eventuality. Before that date a special Regency Bill was always necessary whenever a Regency was required, whatever the reason.

"After 1937 the position was quite clearly stated: The Regent was to be the next person in succession to the Throne who was of full age and in other respects capable of succeeding.

"It is argued by the constitutional pundits . . . that for the Duke of Edinburgh to be named as Regent would accord with the precedent of 1840, when Prince Albert was named Regent in the event of anything happening to Queen Victoria.

"But there is no exact parallel here. For in 1840 Queen Victoria was the only member of the Royal Family suitable for the Throne. All the others were unsuitable, for one reason or another. In fact, most unsuitable.

"Today it certainly could not be urged that those next in succession to Princess Margaret were unsuitable."

Mr. Wintour ended his article by saying that the proposed changes "would nullify and destroy the whole principle that governs the royal succession in Britain—the principle of heredity.

"The British Monarchy owes much of its strength to the simplicity of that guiding theme. Why should it be altered now?"

In the Labour Party's newspaper, the *Daily Herald,* the outspoken political columnist, Michael Foot, under the headline "Regency Humbug!" wrote

"The new Regency Bill will replace the Regency Act of 1937. What did that Act say? It was introduced by Sir John Simon (now Lord Simon), who is regarded by some people as the greatest lawyer of the century. And the main argu-

ment of Sir John was that his Act would make any more
Regency Acts in the future unnecessary.

"Sir John put the case with all the brilliance which had
restored so many suspected criminals to his friends and relatives. . . . Only three men raised their voices in opposition.
. . . How Sir John flayed them for their presumption.

"Why, if the 1937 Regency Act was good, is a new one to
be put in its place?"

Mr. Foot said the opponents in 1937 were James Maxton,
leader of the Independent Labour Party, George Buchanan,
his redoubtable lieutenant, and William Gallacher, the
Communist. Mr. Foot asked:

"Why make a monkey of Sir John and elevate the great
and good Jimmy Maxton as the matchless authority on our
monarchical system?"

The *Times* approved the proposed change, suggesting that
all that was at stake was the "business affairs" of a child if his
mother should die and that it was better to leave them in the
hands of the father than hand them over to an aunt. And then
the *Times* added that the choice of the Queen's understudy
is "a matter for the Queen and her family . . . to settle for
themselves, with the counsel and aid of all her constitutional
advisers."

Thundered Aneurin Bevan's *Tribune:* "Rub your eyes
and read again. Haven't they got any history books at the
*Times* office? Both the succession and the Regency are matters which Parliament has decided. Several battles, both inside and outside the Commons, have been fought on the
point. The best service the Government can do to the Royal
Family is to drop this Regency Bill. Indeed, the Regency Act
of 1937 was passed for the express purpose of making the
selections automatic and the controversies dead. So why dig
them all up again?"

But not all the criticism of the proposed new Regency Bill
was confined to the "succession" problem. In London there

was a deep undertow of nervousness and grumbling in the starchy back benches of the Conservative Party—men who are properly silent in public and more often than not, violently articulate in private. Although the handsome, gregarious Prince Philip was taking his job energetically and seriously and becoming increasingly popular with the public, he was not, and still is not, universally beloved by the English aristocracy. They rather distrust him; his politics are comparatively liberal; he has played loose with some of the stuffier conventions of the palace; he is a foreigner—a Greek prince naturalized as a British citizen; but, above all, he is a Battenberg, a nephew of the dashing, controversial Admiral of the Fleet, Earl Mountbatten of Burma and his equally controversial wife, Edwina—the friend of Nehru.

Battenberg, a name to reckon with in medieval Germany, had come alive again, after five centuries of obscurity, by the time that Prince Louis of Battenberg, half German and half Polish, married Queen Victoria's granddaughter. He moved to England, became First Sea Lord of the Admiralty and an intimate adviser to Victoria, Edward VII, and George V. In World War I the Battenbergs translated their German name directly into English: Mountbatten.

Louis' son, the present Lord Louis, Earl Mountbatten of Burma, took up where his father left off, joined the Royal Navy, went around the world with his cousin, Edward, the Prince of Wales. He married the commoner granddaughter of the fabulously wealthy Sir Ernest Cassel (a German-Jewish financier) whose money irrigated the Nile Valley, reconstructed Argentina's finances, built railroads in Sweden, refloated China after her disastrous war with Japan in 1894–1895, sponsored the "tuppenny tube" (the forerunner of the present Underground). Sir Ernest left Edwina on his death a large share of a £6 million inheritance.

For three decades Lord Louis (Dickie, to his friends) and Edwina, both brilliant, handsome, and unabashedly extrovert, have made the headlines, salon gossip, friends and enemies throughout the British Commonwealth. After World War I, Lord Mountbatten led the Mayfair set and the British Commandos in World War II. He also won distinction as Supreme Allied Commander in Southeast Asia. Commented the late American General Joe Stilwell who had to deal with Mountbatten: "A nice guy. That's what makes him so dangerous—he turns on the charm like a water faucet." And others have said: "Philip, too, has the Mountbatten charm."

After the war Mountbatten became Viceroy of India and presided over the birth of an independent India, became an ally of Nehru and the Labour Party, and emerged from it all a trusted friend of Winston Churchill.

Never far behind was Edwina. A mingling of German, English, Scottish, Irish, and perhaps even American Indian blood (she claims descent from the Pocahontas), she has shared her husband's limelight and ambitions, his tendency to cultivate the left wing, his love of finery and entertaining. Some of her friendships have jarred social London. Once, when a canvasser for the Labour Party called on them, Lord Mountbatten assured him: "Don't worry about us. It's the servants you want to work on."

Prince Philip, the debonair son of Lord Louis' sister, Alice of Battenberg, and of Prince Andrew of Greece, was ushered into English life as a ward of his Uncle Louis. Some saw the hand of the Mountbattens in the romance which made Philip husband of the heiress presumptive. The wedding night and the first part of the royal honeymoon in 1947 was spent at the Mountbattens' 6,000-acre estate at Broadlands.

In one hundred years the blood of the Battenbergs has risen from obscurity on the banks of the Rhine to the threshold of the most important Throne Room on earth. The next King of England will be a Battenberg.

It is, therefore, not surprising that the Earl of Mountbatten strongly favored the marriage of Princess Margaret to the Earl of Dalkeith. It was already suspected in the inner circles of the royal family that the Princess was in love with her father's Equerry. Such an alliance to a commoner would not be looked upon with favor by either Lord Louis or Edwina. Nothing must tarnish the Crown.

The hostility to the new Regency Bill was not confined to London. In faraway Australia, the powerful Sydney *Sunday Sun* asked: "Why should the twenty-two-year-old Princess of the Royal House of Windsor be superseded and in her place a Mountbatten be nominated."

The bill was debated in Parliament early in November and rushed through both Houses in a few days, it being given the royal assent on November 19. The haste was said to be necessary for the reversal of the position of the Duke of Edinburgh and Princess Margaret to be made before the royal tour to Australia began on November 23.

Hostility from many quarters to a change in the Regency Act of 1937 continued. The criticism could be crystallized as follows: The 1937 Act made the choice of regent as undiscussible as that of the sovereign. Once you become involved in arguments as to who would be the most suitable person for regent you open the possibility in future years for the matter being lobbied and canvassed and becoming the sport of party politics.

There would also be the risk of this being used as a precedent for the choice of sovereign. If you are going to pick the best man for regent, why not pick the best man for king? The British Constitution works because it can survive under good, bad, and indifferent sovereigns. With stronger reason it can survive under good, bad, and indifferent regents. In a word, you should no more shop around for your regent than you should for your king.

The ideas of primogeniture and of a hereditary monarchy were devised long ago to prevent unseemly and perhaps bloody quarrels over the succession. Bluntly the critics in Britain and in the Commonwealth countries did not like the new Regency Bill because it tampered with the line of succession. If changes had to be made to permit Princess Margaret to marry a commoner, these critics argued that the regency should pass to the Duke of Gloucester and if the necessity arose to the Princess Royal.

The question of who was to be regent was much more important than, as the *Times* put it, "a business affair" of a father bringing up his son. The sovereign of Great Britain and the Commonwealth wields, among others, these important powers, which a regent would take over:

To recruit or disband the fighting forces.

To sign, or refuse to sign, bills. (The royal signature makes them acts of Parliament.)

To prorogue Parliament.

To appoint, or dismiss, Prime Ministers.

To make law by issuing Orders in Council.

To pardon the legally condemned.

A sovereign is strongest in a time of crisis, when his or her powers can be used most effectively. A resolute sovereign could make a vital difference to affairs by these three decisions: The man called to be Prime Minister; the use to which he (or she) might put the Armed Forces; the emergency laws he (or she) might make or veto. Perhaps in the mid-twentieth century a new stress is laid on the powers of the Crown, though it is long since some of them were exercised. The sovereign is a possible last bulwark against dictatorship. Therefore, it is imperative to consider carefully who, in an emergency, may be the acting sovereign.

And this vital question of the succession to the throne became an all-important factor two years later when the hour of decision was reached as to whether Princess Margaret should marry Group Captain Townsend.

At this point it is, therefore, necessary to examine the legal and theological difficulties and implications involved by such a possible marriage, together with the historical background of both aspects.

# The Law

"I HAVE REACHED THIS DECISION ENTIRELY ALONE. . . ." THESE were the words of Princess Margaret in her dramatic communiqué from Clarence House on the night of October 31, 1955. For days it had been stressed by court officials, politicians and, of course, prelates, that the sad, harassed young Princess was not being subjected to outside pressures. In a word, she was completely free to make up her own mind as to whether she wished to marry Group Captain Peter Townsend or not.

But all these statements were really only half truths. In fact, the Princess was in a mental and physical strait jacket. She was not free to marry whom she liked. She never had been. And she is not free to do so today.

What were the impediments to her marrying whom she wished? The first and most important was the Royal Marriages Act. Its provisions required the consent of the Queen to the marriage of the Princess. This act is not a measure whose origin and purpose are widely known. Passed in 1772 in the reign of George III, it was forced through Parliament in a fit of temper by the King.

In whatever Valhalla rest the spirits of Fox and Burke, the great political masters of the eighteenth century, their roars of Augustan laughter, as they contemplated the absurdities being enacted in those near-crisis autumn days of 1955, must have disturbed the peace of their solemn surroundings. One can almost catch the loud precipitate tones of Burke, calling with exulting glee, "I told you so."

Almost everyone agreed in 1955 that this act should be repealed because it was out of keeping with mid-twentieth-century thinking and practice. Sir Anthony Eden, the Prime

Minister, after the Margaret-Townsend crisis had been re-
solved, promised in the House of Commons that the Government would consider its amendment. Soon Eden was im-
mersed in the Suez crisis and then had to resign because of
ill health. Nothing has been done.

What was thought of the act when it was debated in Parliament in 1772 was coarsely but not ineptly said by the
grandson of Molly Lepell: "The Bill gives leave to the
Princes of the Blood to lie with our wives but forbids them
to marry our daughters."

Once the act became law, George III and his wife, Queen
Charlotte, certainly applied its provisions with rigor.

There is evidence that Queen Charlotte, who came from
the pompous but diminutive royal house of Mecklenburg-
Strelitz, was fixed in the notion that royals—to use the old
eighteenth-century phrase—must only marry royals. But the
bill, as we shall see, was the responsibility of the King.

In the mid-twentieth century in Britain and the Commonwealth there may still be a case for the marriages of princes
and princesses being questions of both family and public concern. I feel, however, that the terms of the act in question
find no support among the people, and no justification in
principle.

Because it was applied in the case of Princess Margaret, it
is of both historical and public interest to take a close look
at its royal author and its iniquitous provisions, as well as
why the author thought such an act was necessary.

First let us take a look at George III, a man of complicated
and uncanny personality. Because he liked to potter about
his estates at Windsor he was half-contemptuously, half-affec-
tionately given the epithet of Farmer George.

Lecky gave it as his opinion that this king inflicted more
profound and enduring injuries upon his country than any
other modern English king.

In his youth George was described as lethargic, but no one
could say he was lethargic when he became King. He once

admitted that "his memory being a good one ... what he did not *forget* he could not *forgive*"—a point he illustrated by his grim declaration that he would not admit Fox to his councils, "even at the hazard of civil war." His mother was constantly whispering: "George, be a king," in contrast to his grandfather's dependence on the Whig oligarchy.

His first action on ascending the throne on October 25, 1760, showed his determination to "be a king." Dismissing Pitt, who had come to announce his accession, to "await his pleasure," the King consulted none of his ministers on the speech to be addressed to the Council, but only his "dearest friend," the Earl of Bute. In a bid to win the affection of the public, he said: "Born and bred in this country, I glory in the name of Britain." But the appeal fell flat largely because he said Britain instead of England.

Soon after his accession, George fell in love with Lady Sarah Lennox, the youngest daughter of the Duke of Richmond. On many mornings he had been seen riding along the Kensington Road so that he could see his loved one haymaking in the broad meadow in front of Holland House.

Lady Sarah was a lovely girl of fifteen when George III became King and there is no doubt he was planning to marry her. But Sarah hurt his pride by a flirtation with Lord Newbottle, who had made love to all the girls. Actually Newbottle was much in love with Lady Caroline Russell, the Duke of Bedford's daughter. Lady Sarah was trying to get him from Lady Caroline.

This presented the Princess-Dowager of Wales and the Earl of Bute with a weapon, as they had other plans for George. Sarah's flirtation was magnified. Yet in spite of the flirtation the King seemed as much enamored as ever when Sarah went to St. James's for his birthday party on June 4. Horace Walpole, that great reporter of the period, wrote to Lady Ailesbury: "The birthday exceeded the splendour of Haroun al Raschid and the Arabian Nights ... do you remember where a prince has eight statues of diamonds, which he overlooks because he fancies he wants a ninth, and to his great surprise, the ninth proves to be pure flesh and blood? . . . Somehow or other, Lady Sarah is the ninth statue; and you will allow has better white and red than if she was made of pearls and rubies."

Nor is it surprising that Sarah inflamed the King's passions. Lord Holland wrote of his young sister-in-law that her beauty was not easily described, otherwise than by saying that she had the finest complexion, most beautiful hair, and the prettiest person that ever was seen, with a sprightly and fine air, a pretty mouth and remarkably fine teeth and excess of bloom for her cheeks, little eyes—but this was not describing her, for her beauty was a peculiarity of countenance, that made her at the same time different from and prettier than any other girl he had ever seen.

The King was certainly deeply in love. The reason for his break with Sarah could have been her flirtation with Newbottle but the real reason may probably be found in his fear of the Whig bondage which had lasted since James II had abdicated, a bondage which George had been brought up to believe it was his royal task to break. Marriage with Lady Sarah would have kept him in thralldom to the Whig oligarchy.

George turned away from Sarah. He sacrificed *love* for *duty*.

It is a fascinating historical "if" to speculate what might have happened if George, instead of marrying one of those "foggy" German princesses, as Charles II used to call them, had wedded the great-granddaughter of Charles II himself. Would we be incorrect in saying that there would have been no Royal Marriages Act? The narrative as it continues may provide the answer.

A marriage was arranged with Princess Charlotte of Mecklenburg-Strelitz. Lady Sarah was piqued. She wrote to her dearest friend, Lady Susan Fox-Strangways: "My disappointment did not affect my spirits above an hour or two, I believe. I did not cry, I assure you, which I believe you will, as I know you were more set upon it than I was. *The thing I am most angry at is looking like a fool.*" But if she felt a fool it did not stop her from accepting George's consolation prize to be a bridesmaid at the wedding. Lady Caroline Russell and Lady Susan Fox-Strangways were also among the ten bridesmaids, but Walpole wrote: "Lady Sarah was by far the chief angel. Nothing ever looked so charming. The King looked mentally absent and never took his eyes off Lady Sarah throughout the ceremony." He showed signs of emotion when the Archbishop of Canterbury intoning the marriage service came to the words—"And as though didst send thy blessing upon Abraham and Sarah, to their great comfort, so vouchsafe to send thy blessing upon these thy servants. . . ."

I wonder what miseries may not have sprung from this King's cowardice and pride in marrying Charlotte and denying himself what an Archbishop of Canterbury in later years was to call "a craving for private happiness," and what miseries and heartaches to the numerous royal persons resulted from the King's decorous domestic life with his Queen.

Henry Frederick, Duke of Cumberland, the twenty-five-year-old brother of King George III, had good cause to squirm. For intimate letters he had written to the young and beautiful Countess of Grosvenor were being read by bewigged counsel in open court. And so grossly ill-spelled and illiterate were they that each tender line was greeted with hoots of derision.

But Richard, the first Earl Grosvenor, was not laughing at the public disgrace of the King's brother. Discovering that the Duke had seduced his wife, he had brought an action for divorce, citing Cumberland as corespondent. Now, for the first time, a prince of the blood royal appeared in a divorce court, held up to ridicule as a royal Lothario.

In court it was proved that Cumberland and the Countess stayed, disguised, at a cheap inn near Eaton Hall. Lord Grosvenor got his divorce and the Duke had £10,000 damages awarded against him by an unsympathetic jury. But even more damaging than this large sum was the revelation, through his letters which were used as evidence, of his deplorable spelling and grammar. A wit quoted Lord Dorset's ballad:

> "To all ye ladies now at land
> We men at sea indite.
> But first would have you understand
> How *hard* it is to write."

Having faced the Court and the jury, the Duke now had to face his brother, the King, and his intensely respectable sister-in-law. Both the King and Queen Charlotte were profoundly shocked, but the King—hoping (in vain, as it turned out) to avoid further scandal—helped the Duke pay the heavy damages.

There were rumors, and they had reached the King's ears, that the Duke had married in secret, Olivia, the daughter of a Reverend James Wilmot. Hardly had the divorce case of the Earl of Grosvenor ceased to be a topic of conversation than the Duke privately married a widow, Mrs. Anne Horton, the daughter of Lord Irnham and the sister of the fire-eating Colonel Luttrell. The lady was perfectly respectable, though it was observed that she had "very amorous eyes with lashes a yard long."

If the Duke had married Olivia, then of course this marriage was bigamous, and there is evidence that the King threatened to expose his brother. But it became a case of diamond-cut-diamond, because there was a strong belief that George himself in 1753—a boy of fifteen—had married a Hannah Lightfoot, the daughter of Matthew Lightfoot, a shoemaker of Execution Dock, Wapping. The story went that when her father died, Hannah was adopted by one of her mother's brothers, Henry Wheeler, who kept a linen draper's shop at the corner of St. James's Market. The young Prince used to notice her as he passed in his sedan chair.

It must be assumed that Cumberland knew of this affair and so if threatened with exposure for bigamy by the King, he in turn threatened his brother, the King. Cumberland was said to have revealed the King's secret to Mrs. Horton.

Anyway, immediately after the marriage ceremony of the Duke and Mrs. Horton, Cumberland drove to St. James's Palace to see the King with a letter containing notice of the wedding. They walked for some time in the garden before he handed the letter to his brother. Placing it in his pocket, George said: "I suppose I need not read it now?"

"Yes, sir," insisted the Duke, "you must read it directly."

The King tore open the letter and turned white with anger. "You fool! You blockhead! You villain!" he stormed. "You had better have debauched all the unmarried girls in England—you had better have committed adultery with all the married women—but this woman can be nothing—she shall never be anything." And so the scene went on.

The King ordered his brother abroad and had published in the London *Gazette* that any who "choose to wait upon the Duke and the new Duchess" would no longer be received at Court.

Meanwhile the King had other troubles. His youngest sister, Caroline Matilda—married at the age of fifteen to the crazy King of Denmark—had been arrested and imprisoned following an affair with her Prime Minister, Struensee. Another sister, the Princess of Brunswick, was unhappy with her husband, a man of many mistresses.

And his favorite brother, William Henry, Duke of Gloucester, was constantly in the company of Maria, Dowager Countess of Waldegrave, an illegitimate daughter of Sir Edward Walpole by a milliner's apprentice.

Well might Horace Walpole write: "Such an accumulated succession of mortifications has seldom fallen on a Royal Family in so short a space. They seemed to have inherited the unpropitious star of the Stuarts, from whom they are descended, as well as their Crown."

The King's ministers advised him to keep the news of Cumberland's marriage from his mother, the Princess-Dowager, who, though she would not admit it, and bore her suffering in silence, was dying of cancer of the throat. But the King declared: "My mother will know everything and it is better that I break it to her by degrees."

Anger and grief overwhelmed the Princess-Dowager when she was told of the family misfortunes. Turning to the wall she prayed for death. She broke off all communications with the Duke of Cumberland and forbade her servants and remaining children to mention the name of her daughter Matilda.

The events certainly hastened the death of the Princess-Dowager, who died in February, 1772.

A fortnight after his mother's death, the King instructed the Tory Prime Minister, Lord North, to introduce legislation making it illegal for members of the royal family to marry without the consent of the reigning sovereign. A historian might find some difficulty in recalling an act of Parliament whose origins were more transitory or more discreditable than were those of the Royal Marriages Act—known at the time as the King's Bill. He might also find it difficult to recall a measure which had been received with fiercer, more justified, or more protracted opposition.

Walpole used words about the bill not dissimilar to the historic phrase of Winston Churchill nearly two centuries later: "Never was an act passed *against* which so much and *for* which so little was said."

The King's message to both Houses of Parliament relative to marriages of the royal family was sent down on February 20, 1772. It stated that the King was desirous "that the right of approving all marriages in the royal family (which ever has belonged to the kings of this realm, as a matter of public concern) may be effectual"; and recommending to their consideration the expediency of guarding "the descendants of his late Majesty George II" (other than the issue of princesses

married into foreign families), from marrying without the
the approbation of the king.

That same day Charles James Fox resigned from his post
as junior Lord of the Treasury. This defection alarmed Lord
North, as possibly the threatened defection of Lord Salisbury
alarmed Sir Anthony Eden when the Margaret-Townsend
crisis arose. In a letter to Lord Ossory, Charles Fox stated: "I
should not have resigned at this moment merely on account
of my complaints against Lord North, if I had not determined to vote against this Royal Family Bill, which, in place,
I should be ashamed to do."

Walpole in his journals noted that: "Lord North and the
ministers were ridiculously alarmed, and so much terrified by
the defection of Mr. Fox and the disapprobation of others,
that they obtained a modification of the Act, and brought it
in the next day with an alteration, exempting Princes (or
Princesses) from positive prohibition of marriage after twenty-
five years of age, and enabling them, after leaving a declaration for a year before the Privy Council, to marry, unless
Parliament make an objection."

Horace Walpole, uncle of the Duchess of Gloucester, was
extremely well informed on all the machinations surrounding the bill, and he correctly saw, as did all intelligent parlia-
mentarians, that this clause was merely "a chicane to make a
seeming softening without a real difference."

In using this word he was doubtless thinking of those lines
from Pope which hit off the two professions which have ever
been the most solid buttresses of this act:

> "Morality by her false guardians drawn
> (Chicane in furs, and Casuistry in lawn)."

The King went to great lengths to insure the passage of the
bill. Throughout the debates he scribbled notes to Lord
North. He even used the ominous words, "I shall remember
defaulters."

On February 26 the bill was read a second time in the

Princess Margaret at Covent Garden, October 27, 1955

KEYSTONE PRESS AGENCY, LTD.

*Above.* The day the announcement was made. Peter Townsend arrives at Clarence House, October 31, 1955. *Below.* Peter Townsend at Uckfield House, Sussex, November 1.

KEYSTONE PRESS AGENCY, LTD.

Lords. The debates centered around questions to the judges as to whether the King was entrusted by law with the care and approbation of the marriage of the descendants of the late King George II, other than the present King's own children. Such slow procedure did not please the King. He wrote:

> "Lord North—I cannot say the management of the Debate in the House of Lords has edified me. I hope there will be a meeting tomorrow to settle the mode of proceeding on Friday."

The judges gave it as their unanimous opinion, delivered by Mr. Baron Smythe: "We are all of the opinion that the care and approbation of the marriages of the King's children and grandchildren and of the presumptive heir to the Crown (other than the issue of princesses married into foreign families) do belong to the Kings of the Realm; but to what other branches of the Royal Family such care and approbation extend *we do not find precisely determined.*"

The question was then put: "To what other degrees of kindred and to what ages of the contracting parties does such right of approbation extend?"

This was objected to and not put to the judges.

The question of whether the law gives care and approbation of the marriages of all descendants, other than the issue of princesses married to foreign princes, was not put to the judges.

When the bill was debated in Committee on Monday, March 2, the Marquis of Rockingham lamented the speed with which the measure was being driven through Parliament. He thought the bill went too far in giving the King the care and approbation of all marriages of all the descendants of George II. Allowing his imagination of royal fertility to run away with itself, he thought those descendants might "amount to many thousands."

The Lord Chancellor, Lord Thurlow, defended every clause, every sentence, every syllable, in fact, every letter in the bill. Not, perhaps, surprising because he had a major share in drafting it. He would accept no amendments. He concluded, "The King cannot make bad use of this power, because Parliament would punish any minister who advised the King ill."

The Bishop of Oxford had feared for the moral danger of preventing members of the royal family marrying from inclination; but Warburton, the Bishop of Gloucester, suggested they could enjoy themselves *without* marriage. An Earl promptly retorted he would now drive with his chariot and liveries to places where previously he had been in the habit of going incognito.

On Tuesday, March 3, the bill was passed in the Lords after a long debate by 90 votes to 26.

But two protests were registered. Among the peers signing the first was the Marquis of Abergavenny. It was this family that was to play a central part in the Townsend-Margaret drama in 1955. Because of this strange coincidence, it is worth recording the terms of the protest: "It seems indecent to the Royal Family to suppose they will not be arrived at the age of discretion as soon as the lowest subject of the realm and we cannot conceive but they may be as capable of choosing a wife at the age of twenty-one as of being entrusted with the Regency of the Kingdom, of which by law they are at that age capable." These words applied, of course, to the case of Princess Margaret nearly two hundred years later.

The next day, Wednesday, March 4, the bill was brought down from the Lords. The Opposition tried to delay matters by moving that the measure should be printed. This move failed, and on the following Monday, March 9, it was ordered for a second reading.

No strangers were admitted to the Chamber, even the peers being locked out of their gallery. It was a long and violent debate, the words "cruelty" and "tyranny" frequently occurring. An adjournment at two o'clock in the morning was refused by the Government. At three o'clock the Opposition walked out.

Before it was light, Lord North had penned an account of the debate and sent it across to the King in St. James's Palace. At eight o'clock the King replied:

> "Lord North—Nothing can be more pleasant than Your Account of the Debate. I am desirous of knowing more of it, therefore, I wish You would call here at any time that suits You this Evening."

Later on that day the House went into Committee. A remarkable speech was made by Lord Folkestone, son of Lord Radnor, whose name had headed one of the protests of the dissentient Lords. It had been drafted by Burke, and fastened on the right of a member of the royal family to marry after twenty-five, independently of the sovereign, and the subsequent sentence "unless both Houses of Parliament expressly declare their disapprobation." With prescience the protest pointed out that this would lay "great difficulties on future Parliaments."

We shall see later in this narrative the dilemma in which Princess Margaret was placed by this clause, when she sought the advice of the Queen's Minister, Sir Anthony Eden, when he went to Balmoral in August, 1955.

Lord Folkestone claimed that the bill was "built upon such false principles, and contains so many exceptionable positions," that he thought it ought to be immediately rejected. Its preamble was inadmissible because it contained a "new and unheard of prerogative, a right to the care and approbation of the marriages of the Royal Family as ancient and acknowledged."

Later Lord Folkestone said: "If we compare the notorious occasion of introducing this Bill . . . with another part of the preamble, we shall find a doctrine, which I cannot help thinking the representative of the people, that people, whom I think obliquely insulted by the words, will unitedly oppose, we shall find it is the opinion of the minister speaking in His Majesty's message, that an alliance of a subject with a branch of the Royal Family is *dishonourable* to the Crown."

Then Lord Folkestone added significantly: "I shall be told this restraint lasts only to twenty-five; I wish it may then cease. The power of restraining is transferred to the Parliament.

"Now, not to speak disrespectfully, or even suppose the ductility of modern Parliaments; figure to yourself, Sir, some future one under the influence of the Crown, and to give my argument greater scope, let it not be unconstitutional influence, but such as arises from a series of popular acts, by which we will suppose he has ingratiated himself with his subjects, indeed so much as to be, I will say, improperly beloved by them. Will a Parliament at such a time, if at any, fail to disapprove of a choice known to be disapproved of by the sovereign, and which by the direction of this Bill, cannot be known to be so?"

I do not wish to anticipate in detail the events which led up to the crisis of the Margaret-Townsend affair in the autumn of 1955, but this is a convenient point to draw some conclusions from Lord Folkestone's remarkable speech which had a significant bearing on the issue under discussion.

Folkestone used the words an "alliance . . . *dishonourable* to the Crown." An alliance between Peter Townsend and Princess Margaret was so judged by those around the Court in 1955. Townsend was a *commoner,* but more important he was *divorced.* A marriage, such as was proposed, would, in the opinion of the Queen's advisers, bring *dishonor* to the Crown.

But the Queen could only veto a marriage while Princess Margaret was under twenty-five.

What was her position then? As Folkestone said: She was in the hands of Parliament. And as he so rightly pointed out: Would Parliament approve of an alliance which was *disap-*

*proved* by the Monarch? Folkestone did not think so. Nor do I think that Parliament would have approved of Princess Margaret's marrying Peter Townsend if she had refused to give up most of her royal prerogatives.

I will not dwell further at this stage with these very controversial aspects of the proposed Margaret-Townsend alliance. But as the story unfolds we shall see; I submit that my conclusions are correct.

In spite of every effort of oratory in the Commons in those March days of 1772, including some fierce and brilliant speeches by Fox, in one of which he asked if the dignity of the Crown depended on the marriages of the royal family, the bill was passed. At the last moment, Burke and Fox made a bid to restrict the provisions of the bill to the reign of George III. This amendment was defeated amid scenes of great excitement by a narrow majority of 18, which might have been no more than 6 if 12 of the minority voters had not been locked out of the division lobby.

The King was delighted. At six o'clock on March 24, he wrote:

> "Lord North—the finding you have so early this day finished the Royal Marriages Bill gives so much satisfaction, and I shall at all times with pleasure reflect the Spirit and Zeal you have shown in conducting it through the different stages."

But others were less pleased. The leading article of the *Public Advertiser* on March 24 said:

> "The Royal Marriage Bill has been passed to the Expense of two British Baronies, five Irish ditto, one Advancement from ditto to an Irish Earldom, one Blue Ribbon, three Red ones, the Baronetage, three Reversionary Patent Places, Twenty Five Thousand Pounds in occasional gratuities, besides innumerable promises of Lottery Tickets. In so very interesting and constitutional light is this Bill seen by our worthy representatives."

The Town had its own epithet:

> "Quoth Dick to Tom, 'This Act appears
>     Absurd as I'm alive:
> To take the Crown at eighteen years,
>     The wife at twenty-five.
> The mystery how shall we explain,
>     For sure as Dowdeswell said,
> "Thus early if they're fit to reign,
>     They must be fit to wed"?'
> Quoth Tom to Dick, 'Thou art a fool,
>     And little knowest of life,
> Alas! 'tis easier far to rule
>     A kingdom than a wife.' "

Six months after the passing of the act a new sensation broke upon the country. The Duke of Gloucester, induced by sympathy for his brother Cumberland, informed the King that he, too, had been secretly married . . . that Lady Waldegrave had, in fact, been his wife for six years.

Gloucester was immediately banished from the Court, just as Cumberland had been, and the King directed an inquiry into the validity of the marriage. A silent and reserved man with none of the brutishness of Cumberland, Gloucester had become enamored of Maria, Lady Waldegrave, soon after his twenty-first birthday in 1764.

Maria, who had been left a fortune and three children by her late husband, was hardly the woman to marry the King's brother; yet she was too considerable to become his mistress. But the obstacles to his love only served to make the Duke's passion more violent.

Threats, advice, and warnings were in vain and on September 6, 1766, they were married in the drawing room of her house in Pall Mall by her personal chaplain, Dr. Morton.

During the years that followed they guarded their secret jealously, though in public his manner to her was always that of a husband to his wife. And they let the gossips chatter.

George III was as angered with Gloucester's prior offense

as with Cumberland's private marriage. Though acknowledg-
ing the marriage was legal, he refused to receive the new
Duchess at Court, and as a result the couple spent considerable time abroad. In later years the King was reconciled with
Gloucester, but he never forgave Cumberland.

What was really George III's motive in forcing a reluctant
Parliament to pass the Royal Marriages Act? We are entitled
to ask this most pertinent question, as the provisions of the
act are undoubtedly out of keeping with our present democratic conception of the monarchy.

There is no doubt that although the act was occasioned
specifically by the marriage of one of George III's brothers,
it was inspired by the King's large ideas of the power of the
Crown for, as was said in the debate on the measure, "the
fruit tasted of the tree of prerogative."

Those last words seem sufficient grounds to justify scrap-
ping the act.

                    *       *       *

"No one is compelled to be a Churchman," declared the
Report of the Joint Committee of the Convocations of Canterbury and York on the Church, Marriage, and Divorce,
issued in 1935. "There are many Englishmen who do not pro-
fess to be Churchmen."

That is true, except in the case of one Englishman (or
woman). The sovereign is compelled, so long as the Church
is Established, to be a member of the Church of England.
And as the members of the royal family, under the provisions
of the Royal Marriages Act, have to seek the monarch's authority to marry until they reach the age of twenty-five, each
member of the royal family is, therefore, subject to the rules
of the Anglican Church until that age—whether he agrees
with them or not.

Thereafter, the authority governing their marriages passes,
as we have seen, to Parliament, the members of the two
Houses. Lords and Commons, being composed of men and

women of differing creeds and denominations, in consequence, have differing views on marriage, divorce, and re-marriage.

The provision of the act governing members of the royal family after they have reached the age of twenty-five has never been tested. But, as we shall later see, if it had been tested in the case of Princess Margaret, it was by no means certain that Parliament would not have vetoed her marriage to Group Captain Townsend.

If the law of the land permits divorce and remarriage, the provisions of the Royal Marriages Act are absurd.

# The Church

As we have seen from the preceding pages, the immediate stumbling block to Princess Margaret's marrying Peter Townsend in 1953 was the outdated Royal Marriages Act of 1772. As the Princess was not twenty-five and so required her sister's permission to wed, the Queen withheld it as temporal Governor of the Church of England because Townsend was a divorced man.

But what is the Anglican Church's record on marriage, divorce, and the remarriage of divorced persons? It might be described as the ebb and flow of a doctrinal tide and the uncertain swell of a disciplinary sea.

The Church of England, as we recognize it today, arose from the desire of Henry VIII to marry Anne Boleyn. The *causes* that led to that wish do not concern us. But there is an erroneous impression that the King wished to *divorce* Catherine of Aragon. What he sought was an annulment of his marriage because it was not a valid marriage, his wife having been the wife for four months of his dying brother Arthur. That marriage certainly was not consummated: Prince Arthur was not fifteen and Catherine barely sixteen when they were married in St. Paul's in November, 1501. By April Catherine was a virgin widow.

Not long afterward Henry VII lost his wife, and then to the consternation of Catherine's mother, Isabella, proposed that he should marry his widowed daughter-in-law. In the end Catherine was betrothed to Arthur's younger brother Henry in 1503 when the Prince was only twelve years old, after Pope Julius II granted a bill of dispensation for the marriage. Henry and Catherine were married in June, 1509,

137

seven weeks after Henry VIII's accession to the throne. They were crowned together a fortnight later.

By 1526 Henry was infatuated with Anne, the younger sister of his former mistress, Mary Boleyn. He asked Pope Clement VII to declare his marriage with Catherine null and void. The Pope refused.

Thus began the long battle between the Pope and the King.

The King opened his offensive against Rome by discovering that Cardinal Wolsey had broken the statute of Praemunire, which made the right of presentation to church benefices belong to the King's Court, made any juridical interference by Rome illegal, and called for the forfeiture of all property and possessions by anyone aiding Rome to override this authority. Wolsey had been exercising the legatine authority which the Pope at Henry's request had conferred upon him. In consequence of this move by the King, Wolsey forfeited all his property to the Crown. He was sentenced to death but anticipated the headsman's ax by dying while on his way to the Tower.

Henry and his skillful lawyers then discovered that all the clergy of England were guilty of Praemunire because they had obeyed the legatine authority of Wolsey. An information was filed against them in the King's Bench, and in January, 1531, the Convocation of Canterbury met to sue for pardon. This was granted in return for a fine of £100,000 and assent to the formula of royal supremacy.

The words of the great surrender were:

> "We acknowledge His Majesty to be the singular protector, only and supreme lord, and, so far as the law of Christ will allow, supreme head of the Church of England and Clergy."

The Convocation of York followed suit, paying £18,000, and subscribed to the formula.

With the death of old Wareham, the Archbishop of Canterbury, in 1532, the King appointed Thomas Cranmer Archbishop.

The King privately married Anne Boleyn at the beginning of 1553 and two months later the Convocation was asked to declare the validity of the marriage of Arthur and Catherine and to deny the power of the Pope to grant a dispensation for marriage with the widow of a deceased brother. Cranmer on May 29, sitting as president of the Archiepiscopal Court at Dunstable, set aside Henry's marriage with Catherine as null and void, and declared the marriage with Anne Boleyn valid. Following a series of enactments, the breach with Rome was complete.

We need not follow the infamy of Henry's other marriage affairs. However, on the death of the King, the Archbishop, possibly to clear his conscience, led a movement to make the Church of England conform with Continental Protestantism. The Reformers rejected the sacramental theory of marriage.

The Church of England has made no changes in Canon Law on divorce since 1603.

Canon 107 declares:

> "In all sentences for Divorce, Bond to be taken for not marrying during each other's Life.

> "In all sentences pronounced only for divorce and separation *a toro et mensa* [from bed and board], there shall be a caution and restraint inserted in the act of the said sentence, that the parties so separated shall live chastely and continently; neither shall they, during each other's life, contract matrimony with any other person. And, for the better observation of this last clause, the said sentence of divorce shall not be pronounced until the party or parties requiring the same have given good and sufficient caution and security into the court, that they will not in any way break or transgress the said restraint or prohibition."

This Canon is the rock on which the opponents of the remarriage of divorced persons is based. But it is followed immediately by Canon 108 which declares:

"The Penalty for Judges offending in the premises.

"And if any judge, giving sentence of divorce or separation, shall not fully keep and observe the premises, he shall be, by the Archbishop of the province, or by the Bishop of the diocese, suspended from the exercise of his office for the space of a whole year; and the sentence of separation, so given contrary to the form aforesaid, shall be held void to all intents and purposes of the law as if it had not at all been given or pronounced."

By the removal of matrimonial jurisdiction from the ecclesiastical courts to civil courts, this Canon has been rendered obsolete. Why, therefore, should the laity suppose that Canon 107 is not equally obsolete?

But there are further snags. The Canons were framed in Latin. The translations, according to the Reverend J. V. Bullard, the Proctor of the Convocation of York in 1606, were often quite inaccurate.

In Canon 107 the Latin heading *"Separatis, eorum altero superstite, nova copula interdicta,"* is translated "In all sentences for divorce, Bond to be taken for not marrying during each other's Life." But the Latin literally translated says: "A new tie is forbidden to *separated* parties, either of them being alive." In this Canon the Latin explicitly refers to *"separationem tori et mensae,"* and again to *"sententia separationis,"* whereas the English inserts *"divorce and* separation" and on the second occasion translates *"separatio"* as "divorce." That this cannot be explained away by a looseness of translation which considers *"divortium"* and *"separatio"* interchangeable is suggested by Canon 108, for here we have both in English and Latin an apparently express statement that divorce and separation are not the same: *"Sententiam separationis, seu divortii."* True, it might be maintained that *"seu"* is used with the sense *"seu potius,"* thus making *"separatio"* and *"divortium"* identical, but such an ambiguity is unusual in ecclesiastical Latin.

It is clear that Canon 107 forbids the remarriage of separated parties, but it is by no means so clear that the Latin and authoritative version forbids the remarriage of divorced parties.

So the Anglican clergy today who refuse to remarry even innocent parties in divorce are relying on a collection of obsolete weapons. Of course, they prefer to base their case on the words of the marriage service to prove that the Church of England is committed to the doctrine of the indissolubility of matrimony. In the marriage service both the parties, in phrases of singular poignancy and beauty, take a solemn vow before the minister (described in the Common Prayer Book as a priest) joins their hands, with the words "Those whom God hath joined together let no man put asunder." The intention, of course, is that such a solemnization of matrimony is to bless and confirm sacramental union between the man and the woman. But it seems rather doubtful in the knowledge of the circumstances in which the Book of Common Prayer was put together that the compilers were animated by the same spirit.

The vows made in the Anglican rite by the parties must logically be held to exclude *"separatio"* if they are to be accepted as final and binding:

> "I take thee to my wedded wife (or husband), to have and to hold from this day forward, for better for worse, for richer for poorer, in sickness and in health, to love and to cherish, till death us do part, according to God's holy ordinance; and thereto I plight thee my troth."

But the declaration of the priest, "Those whom God hath joined together let no man put asunder," is nullified by any acceptance in the future of the right of an ecclesiastical court to grant *"separatio a mensa et toro"* and cannot therefore be recognized as more than a pious ejaculation testifying to an ideal. Once the vows of the parties have been broken and the declaration of the priest has been mocked by the acceptance of judicial separation, nothing remains in the English marriage service itself which affirms the impossibility of remarriage.

That ejaculation of the priest and those solemn vows provide a tempting argument to use with uninformed laymen who are always impressed by it; but it is putting the marriage service on the same level as a solemn vow to abstain from alcohol or smoking. The breaking of such a vow is a *sin,* but a priest could absolve a man from such a vow. A priest cannot unmarry a man who has been validly married. The Church cannot do it.

On the question of sacraments, the Catechism states positively that Christ has ordained two sacraments only, as generally necessary to salvation, Baptism and the Supper of the Lord. Those five commonly-called sacraments—confirmation, penance, order, matrimony, and extreme unction—are, according to the Articles of Religion, not to be counted as sacraments of the gospel, having grown partly from the corrupt interpretation of the teaching of the apostles, and being partly states of life allowed in the Scriptures, but having no visible sign of ceremony ordained of God as baptism and the Lord's supper have.

At an early date the Ecclesiastical Courts had complete jurisdiction over all matters relating to marriage and its dissolution. The right of appeal lay with the Pope. After the relations between Church and State were placed on a new basis in the reign of Henry VIII, the Crown became the supreme authority. The right of appeal to Rome was abolished by the Statute of Appeals in 1533.

After the Reformation these Courts continued to exercise matrimonial jurisdiction and the principal relief granted included decrees of nullity, decrees for restitution of conjugal rights in cases of desertion, and decrees of divorce *a mensa et toro,* which we should now call decrees of judicial separation on the grounds of adultery, cruelty, and unnatural offenses. But the Courts had no power to grant divorce as we understand it today.

From the seventeenth century until 1857, the only means of setting aside a valid marriage was by private Act of Parliament. It was an expensive and slow process. There were only 244 such dissolutions between the years 1715 and 1857.

There was one divorce case in the seventeenth century which had a significant bearing on the issue of parties being remarried. It set a precedent.

Henry, a Protestant Duke of Norfolk, married Mary Mordaunt, daughter of Henry, Earl of Peterborough. In 1685 Mary was charged with having committed adultery with St. John Germain, a soldier of fortune and most probably the half-brother of William of Orange. The charge was brought again in 1690 and 1691. Bills were introduced in the House of Lords by the Duke of Norfolk but rejected. A year later, he brought an action in the King's Bench claiming £50,000 damages for "lascivious conversation" with his Duchess. He won but the jury awarded damages and costs for only 100 marks. In 1698 Germain was created a baron. Then, in 1700, a third bill for divorce was brought in and passed by the House of Lords.

On September 15, 1701, the Archbishop of Canterbury granted a license for marriage to "Sir John Germain, of St. James's, Westminster . . . and Lady Mary Mordaunt, of the same, spinster." Soon after they were married.

This case created a precedent whereby the guilty party may be married by license of the Archbishop of Canterbury.

In 1857 Lord Palmerston's Government brought in the Matrimonial Causes Bill. It abolished the jurisdiction of the Ecclesiastical Courts in matrimonial matters and set up a new court—the Court for Divorce and Matrimonial Causes. It also introduced the petition for dissolution of a marriage, which could be presented by a husband or wife on the grounds of adultery and in the wife's case, desertion of two or more years, coupled with adultery, cruelty, and unnatural vice.

When Lord Cranworth, the Lord Chancellor, moved the Bill in the House of Lords in May, 1857, Dr. Sumner, the

Archbishop of Canterbury, declared his intention of voting for the second reading but reserved his right to oppose the final reading unless it included a clause forbidding remarriage to the guilty parties in a suit for divorce.

The Duke of Norfolk, speaking as a Catholic, opposed the Bill, moved a motion that it be referred to a Select Committee to "resolve as to whether the permission for divorced persons to marry again has any warrant in Holy Scripture." The Bishop of St. David's said that he did not believe that "our Blessed Lord intended to take upon himself the character of a temporal legislator." The Bill was regrettable, said the Bishop, but "it was too late to offer any opposition to the measure."

So the Bishop of St. David's with the Archbishop of Canterbury and eleven other prelates voted against the Duke of Norfolk's clause.

The Duke of Norfolk was supported by four Bishops, the most skillful debater being Bishop Wilberforce of Oxford, a staunch High Churchman. But not even he argued that the Church of England taught that marriage was a sacrament.

The Bishop of London went so far as to question the validity of Canon 107 of 1603. He did not believe that by the law of the Church of England marriage was indissoluble.

When the bill was read a third time five bishops voted for it and seven against. The Archbishop who had spoken for it abstained.

At the end of that hot August of the year of the Indian Mutiny the bill was passed in the House of Commons and it became law on January 1, 1858. One concession had been secured: the clergy of the Church of England were not to be penalized either for marrying or refusing to marry divorced persons, but should they refuse they were obliged to give the use of their churches to any clergyman who was willing to perform the service.

I will quote from the *Times* of August 4, 1857, because it

is useful to compare what that newspaper was saying ninety-eight years later.

> "Some of the opponents declare that the most objection-able part of the measure was the permission for remarriage accorded to the guilty party; but the objection, if it has any validity, applies equally to the wrongdoer and to the wronged. No human or Divine law prohibits the marriage of those who may previously have led questionable lives. The real meaning of the dissentients is, not that the divorced woman is unworthy of marriage, but that she is married already; and the same disability must necessarily attach to the injured husband. The pretended desecration of the wed-ding ceremony is a frivolous afterthought. None of the remonstrant clergy would hesitate to bestow the nuptial benediction on a seducer and on his repentant victim. It would be a monstrous abuse of the power if the legislature were to compel a divorced woman to remain the mistress of her paramour."

From 1858 to 1937, adultery remained substantially the sole ground of divorce in England and Wales. In 1937, Mr. A. P. Herbert introduced in the House of Commons a Pri-vate Members Bill which added additional grounds for di-vorce: (1) willful desertion for three years and up; (2) cruelty; and (3) incurable insanity after five years of confinement.

During the second reading debate in the House of Lords, the Archbishop of Canterbury, Dr. Lang, described the bill as being contrary to Christian principles. And yet he did not vote against it.

The year before, Cosmo Lang broadcast on Sunday eve-ning, December 13, 1936—forty-eight hours after King Ed-ward VIII had abdicated. He proclaimed that "even more strange and sad" than the abdication was that the King "should have sought his happiness in a manner inconsistent with Christian principles of marriage."

This was the first unequivocal affirmation by an Anglican Primate of his belief in the indissolubility of marriage since the days of old Archbishop Wareham four hundred years earlier. Dr. Lang, like the Prince, had kissed awake the Sleeping Beauty, bound for four centuries. The Church of England founded upon one divorce was triumphantly refounded upon another.

When we jump nineteen years—the time Princess Margaret was considering marriage to Group Captain Peter Townsend —the new Primate, Dr. Fisher, happily married and the father of six sons, was not slow to voice his views in public. He began soon after the Margaret-Townsend affair started in 1953 by writing a front-page article for the mass circulation newspaper the *Daily Mirror*. Dr. Fisher, I am told, even wrote his own headline, which the newspaper printed in two-inch type:

## THE PRIMATE REPLIES

I will quote only one passage from that article:

> ". . . The words I want to leave with readers are not mine, but Jesus Christ's. He ratified the Seventh Commandment, "Thou shalt not commit adultery" (St. Matthew 5:27). He declared against divorce. "What therefore God hath joined together (i.e., the relationship of life-long marriage), let not man put asunder" (i.e., the parties to the marriage or anyone else) (St. Mark 10:9).

But to show that there is no unanimity on the interpretation of Christ's teachings, I will quote the Dean of St. Paul's, the Very Reverend W. R. Matthews, for the Modern Churchmen's Union:

> "It cannot be denied that there are passages in the Gospel and elsewhere which taken by themselves support the view that marriage in all cases is indissoluble but I believe that careful consideration leads to the conclusion that though our Lord certainly taught that marriage in essence and idea is a lifelong union, He did not intend to legislate on the subject in such a way that divorce is ruled out in every possible case. We have to remember that there is a difference

between the version of His words in Mark and in Matthew and that it was His method to enunciate great principles of conduct rather than rigid rules. . . .

". . . We admit that these cases may be relatively few [where divorce seems best for spiritual welfare of all concerned] but they exist and we cannot think that our Christian faith precludes the remedy which seems the only one for the particular distress. . . .

". . . We cannot think that all marriages entered into after divorce are wrong or other than true marriages and we regret the policy pursued by the Bishops which appears to be aimed at banning all blessing or public prayer on the marriage of divorced persons. We feel that by this rigid and doctrinaire attitude the Bishops cause undeserved distress to some devout church people and often repel those who, having suffered much in a marriage which was a bitter failure, through no fault of their own, are now entering a union which they believe to be the will of God for them and on which they desire the blessing of the Church."

The Modern Churchmen's Union is a society of clergy and laymen founded in 1898 for the advancement of liberal religious thought. The Union believes that the Christian ideal of marriage is best maintained not by the rigorist view that marriage is incapable of dissolution but by the recognition that in certain cases divorce is necessary and permissible as being the lesser of two evils. On the question of remarriage after divorce, the Union takes the view that the resolutions passed in all four houses of Convocation refusing permission for any person to be remarried in Church after divorce is a denial of the legal right of the clergy to exercise their own discretion in the consecrating of such marriages. The Union feels that the Church has no justification for denouncing all such second marriages as being null and void.

In 1955, the year of the finale, the Archbishop spoke to a group of men in the City of London, and his words were printed afterward in pamphlet form.

In the course of his address the Archbishop said that what

Christ says of marriage is "decisive" for Christians. According to the Royal Commission which sat from 1909 to 1912, Christ "intended" to proclaim "the great principle that marriage *ought* to be indissoluble." Every Christian, of course, accepts that. Then the Report says: "There is wide divergence as to whether the ideal thus held up by our Lord was or was not intended by Him to exclude any exceptions." The Archbishop then added: "But so far all agree that 'the ideal or principle of matrimony as monogamous and lifelong union is beyond question.' "

The Archbishop, after discussing Christ's words as quoted in the Gospels, continues: "It is, however, to the possibility of exceptions that attention is generally directed. Is divorce possible? If so on what terms? Was Christ legislating or stating an ideal? Can there be remarriage after divorce at all? If only for some, how are they to be selected?"

Dr. Fisher did not think that Christ was legislating—telling the Church for all time how to deal with marriage discipline. The Church was being left free to find its way according to His will. Then comes what is known as the Pauline Privilege. St. Paul in Corinthians 1, chapter 7, verse 12, said: "To the rest speak I, not the Lord." If a converted Christian husband or wife has an unconverted pagan partner willing to abide, well and good; the one sanctifies the other. If the partner is not willing to abide but departs, let him depart, that is, presumably by divorce. The Archbishop commented that the Church takes St. Paul's words to mean that the converted brother or sister is free to marry again. "I take this as evidence that the Church always had the right to legislate and to make exceptions."

Dr. Fisher continues that some say Christ Himself made exceptions. He was referring to St. Matthew's Gospel, in which the Apostle said that everyone who divorces his wife *save for fornication* makes her an adulteress, and everyone who divorces his wife *save for fornication* and marries another commits adultery.

The Archbishop describes these passages as obscure. "At best if these words mean that anyone who divorces a partner for adultery may marry again, such a single point is of little relevance today, for it is morally unsatisfactory to put so much upon possibly a single act of adultery and to ignore the other causes of marriage breakdown."

But the Archbishop dismisses the theological aspect of the problem and promptly switches to the Church's doctrine. He concludes that the Church has power to legislate. This brings him to where we started to examine the problem: the Canon Law of 1603, which, says Dr. Fisher, allowed no divorce, except *a mensa et toro*—judicial separation. He adds: "It is necessary to emphasise that the Canons of 1603 are still the only Church Laws about divorce and that they do not permit any divorce with the right to remarry."

In a word, the Archbishop is repeating what Dr. Lang said about divorce a few hours after King Edward VIII gave up his throne to marry Mrs. Simpson.

During the intervening nineteen years the Sleeping Beauty has not gone back to sleep and old Wareham may still rest in peace.

One final word on this issue of divorce and remarriage. It will help to explain why many churchmen and women find themselves utterly confused.

In 1937—a year after the abdication—Lord Hugh Cecil urged the Church Assembly to pass a motion calling for an Act of Parliament to enforce the rule against the remarriage by an Anglican churchman of any person whose husband or wife by a former marriage was still alive. It was the Archbishop of Canterbury, Dr. Lang, who suavely succeeded in getting the motion quashed. Lord Hugh Cecil found the situation intolerable.

But the Reverend R. J. E. Boggis (Exeter) "was anxious that the Assembly should express its approval of the remarriage in Church of the innocent party to a divorce." So was Sir Frederick Cripps (Gloucester). So was the Archdeacon of

Dudley. "They were not concerned about the Canon Law of 1603. What concerned them was the fact that in their own lifetime and in the lifetime of their fathers and grandfathers, the Church had again and again sanctioned the marriage of the innocent party." The Bishop of Truro "quoted recorded words of Archbishop Randall Davidson in support of his own contention that the innocent party to a divorce might be re-married in church." The Dean of Hereford was in entire agreement with the Bishop of Truro.

What were the grounds for Dr. Lang's opposing Lord Hugh Cecil's plea? The fear of Disestablishment. He felt that "such a measure as Lord Hugh Cecil desired . . . must involve a most painful clash between the Church and Parliament. He would always be ready to take such a risk . . . if some *large principle were at issue.*"

The most recent authoritative word on the subject of the remarriage of divorced persons was made by the Archbishop of Canterbury, Dr. Fisher, in a television broadcast on Sunday evening, June 29th, 1958.

The statement which he made arose from a decision of the Bishop of Ripon barring from Communion for six months a man who had announced his intention to marry after divorcing his first wife.

The Archbishop said that people involved in divorce must expect "a little discipline" before they could be received back into the Church of England. "The Church's law on divorce," he said, "is not rigid at all. It is sensible."

Dr. Fisher went on: "The Church has one duty and that is to bear witness to what Christ said. And Christ said that marriage was life long. We have to protect that.

"We do it by the only way we can: by saying we will not marry in church anybody who has broken that Christian principle.

"You can go and get married in a registry office perfectly happily. But you cannot ask us, because it would deny our trust.

"That is one side. The other side is the pastoral side. What can we do for people who get into these horrible matrimonial tangles and despair?

"What do we do? We treat them as fellow beings. We try to do what is best for their spiritual welfare.

"And, if we can bring them to see what Christ means and how Christ loves them and what He desires to make fresh in their lives, we can then admit them to Communion quite happily.

"But there has to be a little discipline before that happens."

# The Exile

TWENTY-FOUR HOURS BEFORE PRINCESS MARGARET AND HER mother flew back to London from their tour in Southern Rhodesia, Group Captain Peter Townsend had reported for duty as Air Attaché at the British Embassy in Brussels. So began twenty-eight months of virtual exile from his homeland. He did make occasional visits to London—sometimes on Air Ministry duty and on other occasions to visit Princess Margaret at Clarence House, but he did not see her until the expiration of the agreed period of one year. These visits to the Princess were made in the strictest secrecy—in fact they were carried out almost in the atmosphere of cloak-and-dagger operations. This must have been distasteful in the extreme both to the Princess and to Townsend. And, the question must be asked: Were such tactics really necessary?

In the view of the Court, it was inadvisable that the young couple meet openly, as the question of their marriage was a matter that could not be seriously considered until the Princess was twenty-five and so free from the veto of her sister, the Queen.

Save for a recrudescence of the rumors in the spring of 1955, the "Townsend Affair" was more or less dead until the autumn of that year.

The British Press, on the whole, conducted itself with restraint. This was partly the result of pressure from the palace and partly because of the attitude of the newly-created Press Council.

Before Townsend left England and while the Princess was still in Africa, the brash *Daily Mirror* charged boldly into the heart of the matter by conducting a poll of its readers. Of the 70,142 readers who, the editor of the newspaper claimed, wrote in, 67,907 urged that the Princess be allowed to marry her divorced airman if she wished to; 2,235 said that she should not. The *Daily Mirror*, of course, gave the verdict in the largest possible type on its front page. But it must be pointed out that the readers who took the trouble to vote represented less than one half of 1 per cent of the newspaper's circulation.

However, the new Press Council, perhaps with a desire to impress all that it was to be an important, vigorous body, condemned the *Daily Mirror* poll. At its first meeting, the Council under the chairmanship of Colonel the Honorable J. J. Astor of the *Times*, a resolution was passed:

> "That this meeting of the Press Council, while conscious of the great interest of the public in the lives of members of the Royal Family, strongly deprecates, as contrary to the best traditions of British journalism, the holding by the *Daily Mirror* of a public poll in the matter of Princess Margaret and Group Captain Townsend."

Lord Beaverbrook's London *Evening Standard* promptly asked:

"Where . . . has the *Daily Mirror* sinned? What is the difference, if any, between a leader in the *Manchester Guardian* and a poll of public opinion in the *Daily Mirror?*"

The *Daily Mirror* was quick to defend itself, the editor stating that the "cat" had been put "among the pigeons." "We are accused of a frightful crime of telling the public the things the public is entitled to know," declared the editor. He then went on to say that his newspaper's poll had been accompanied by the "most astonishing hullabaloo" in other sections of the press.

"The *Daily Express*," went on the editor, "referred to 'ridiculous rumours published in America and republished in this country, which have linked his [Townsend's] name with that of Princess Margaret.' The linking of their names, said the *Express*, was a 'nonsensical story.'

"The following day that same newspaper itself quoted American headlines 'Princess Meg's beau banished' and 'Queen "exiles" R.A.F. ace linked to Princess Meg.'

"Meanwhile other newspapers and periodicals have joined in a mighty chorus of 'Tut-tutting.'

"The *Sunday Times* says that the return of the Queen Mother and Princess Margaret from Africa has been marred by an outbreak of ill-conditioned publicity about Princess Margaret's private affairs. It talks of the vulgar and prurient.

"The *Sunday Graphic* is concerned about 'those at home who have been guilty of the grossest dis-service to the Royal Family and nation'—and then smugly announces that it is publishing a series of articles on 'the REAL Princess Margaret.'

"*Time and Tide* refers to 'an inconceivably nauseating display of bad taste and bad manners.'

"These are typical comments. Even Gilbert Harding, whom some regard as the B.B.C.'s master of bad taste, is 'shocked by public comment on the Princess.' He says, quite ridiculously, that 'even if there is substance in the reports it seems to me it is nothing to do with the public.'"

Thundered the *Mirror*:

> NOTHING TO DO WITH THE PUBLIC! THAT'S WHAT SOME PEOPLE THOUGHT ABOUT EVENTS LEADING TO THE ABDICATION OF THE DUKE OF WINDSOR.

And this was not the last to be heard on the question of press treatment of the royal romance. Two years later the Press Council passed another resolution on the subject of royal privacy. After observing that "public interest in the lives of the Royal Family is intense, and rightly so," and that "newspaper comment on Princess Margaret's future is justified," the Council found that "certain papers have offended against good taste and have done a considerable ill-service to the reputation of the Press."

The Princess had then made an appeal, through the

Queen's Private Secretary, to press and public to respect her privacy.

The *Manchester Guardian* commented: "If we in this country behaved with the same good manners towards royalty as they do in Scandinavian countries there would be no need for the appeal. People would treat the members of the Royal Family with the same tolerance and decency that they would think due to themselves. But . . . the public attitude towards royalty has come rather too near idolatry to be easily influenced by such counsels." The newspaper then added that "it would be against human nature for there not to be some vulgar curiosity."

No one would subscribe to the theory that the royal family should submit, as a public duty, to every kind of intrusion by newspapers into their personal doings; they cannot claim the ordinary citizen's rights to privacy, but they have *some* rights. The question is—where exactly should the line be drawn? Where does legitimate reporting and comment pass into "bad taste"?

If opinions on this vary, it is fair to remark that many people continue to read eagerly the very papers they condemn. No doubt feeling a little guilty, they enjoy all the gossip, particularly about the royal family, but get rid of their discomfort by blaming the press with gusto. All newspapers produce for profit. They print what sells.

But there is a last observation that one must make on the question of press publicity. The question of whom Princess Margaret would marry was a matter of public concern if it involved some alteration of the law. And it was assumed that if she carried out her intention of marrying Group Captain Townsend, some legal formalities would have to be complied with. She has a perfect right to marry anyone she chooses. In this respect she still has the freedom of an ordinary woman. But as a member of the royal family, in the line of succession to the throne, she would be making a choice with inescapable public consequences. To marry Group Captain Townsend, the first immediate consequence would be that the marriage would have to be performed outside the Church of England, since Group Captain Townsend is a divorced person, and the Church of England does not countenance the remarriage of divorced persons, even if they are the "innocent party."

Princess Margaret would, therefore, have had to renounce her royal estate, for the Queen is the titular head of the Established Church of England, and it would be improper for the Queen's sister, and possible successor, to enter into a marriage which the Church could not recognize.

So while it is easy to criticize the "vulgar curiosity" of the press, it did have in those fateful years—and still has today—a duty to discuss Constitutional issues. If an error were committed, it was by the officials at Buckingham Palace in not advising the Queen in 1953 that a statement outlining the position was in the best interests of the Crown and of Princess Margaret and Group Captain Townsend.

I mention this aspect of the Margaret-Townsend romance because not for one moment after the Group Captain was exiled to Brussels was the couple permitted a normal atmosphere in which to make their decision. I say *their* decision because it has always been suggested that the only party who had anything to decide was the Princess. But of course Group Captain Townsend, too, had to consider all the implications of a possible marriage. His dilemma was as great as Princess Margaret's. In some respects it was even greater.

Only by a recognition of all these facts, is it possible to appreciate the period of strain which Townsend was called on to endure during his two years' stay in Brussels before the final decision—a period of strain, in a sense, even greater than he had undergone during the Battle of Britain.

For twenty-eight months in Brussels he was under the pitiless magnifying glass of world publicity, forced to endure it, unable to speak. It was during this period that his real strength of character was shown. He was forced to live within himself

—as lonely in the friendly bustling city of Brussels as a man on a Pacific atoll.

And his position was more complicated by the fact that Princess Margaret, whatever may be said to the contrary, had agreed to marry him when she reached the age of twenty-five. But on this, his lips had to be sealed. As he once said in an all-revealing sentence: "The word must come from somebody else."

So on a July day in that summer of 1953, Townsend piled a few bags into his green Ford Zephyr and drove from London down to Dover to catch the cross-Channel car ferry. On landing at Boulogne he drove straight to the British Embassy in the Rue de Spa in Brussels.

Outside the Embassy, some twenty policemen—instead of the usual two—were on duty. As he drove through the high double black doors of the Embassy and stepped out in the courtyard, he was wearing dark glasses and unsmiling. Outside the gates was a crowd of women and typists leaned from windows to catch a glimpse of him.

Twenty minutes after he arrived, the Embassy released a communiqué. It stated:

"Group Captain Peter Townsend, D.S.O., D.F.C., who is replacing Group Captain L. C. Slee, D.S.O., D.F.C., as Air Attaché to the Embassy, on the latter's retirement from the R.A.F., arrived in Brussels today, July 15, to take up his new duties.

"Group Captain Townsend will be staying for some days from his arrival as the guest of the British Chargé d'Affaires, Mr. C. C. Parrott (69 Avenue Churchill)."

Although Townsend acted with painstaking correctitude throughout his stay in Brussels, his being there presented the Embassy with some very special problems.

First, Brussels society decided to lionize him. They showered him with invitations. But he decided he would go only to the social functions it was necessary for him to attend as

Air Attaché. His private choice was for quiet dinner parties with a few close friends. Peter does not like the modern cocktail party. If he is forced to attend one, he usually finds someone he likes and then gets in a corner with him and stays chatting until it is time to leave. In this respect he was probably a disappointment to his Ambassador. Sir Christopher, a bachelor, once told me that he thought Peter would be a great help to him in entertaining after his experience of Court life. Perhaps, in Brussels, Townsend was only interested in self-effacement.

He might have buried himself in hard work. But his post —it has now been abolished—was almost a sinecure. Belgium is a friendly country and there was no need to attempt picking up snippets of military information. It was a job which could have been done by a man with a quarter of Townsend's talent.

When he arrived at the Embassy he found that his staff consisted of one Flight Sergeant. There was a dilapidated black Standard Vanguard for transport. Peter's office was a dreary second-floor back room, furnished with austere service oak furniture and a small carpet. On the walls were pictures of the Queen and the Duke of Edinburgh. The room was reached by climbing first a long red-carpeted grand stairway —which led past the Ambassador's offices—and then continuing on up a narrower stairway, all in all a rather depressing approach. I feel sure that as the months of exile went by, Townsend's feet must have dragged more each morning as he made the ascent to this office.

A few days after arriving in Brussels he went to his first social outing—a dance given by the Ambassador. Peter stayed until after midnight but ignored a dozen of Belgium's most beautiful debutantes. He spent most of the evening smoking and chatting. Already he feared having his name linked with any other woman, and many attempts were made to do so.

The Belgian Premier's twenty-year-old daughter, Maie Louise van Houtte, commented to a reporter: "He is so sad.

We had been saying, 'If Group Captain Townsend does not dance, he must be in love,' and, *voilà*, he does not dance. At dinner he sat between two married ladies. We had wondered why he was so sad and if all the stories of a romance between him and Princess Margaret could be true. I think they must be."

After the initial spate of society invitations began to die away, when it was realized that Townsend had no intention of permitting himself to be lionized, he gave careful consideration as to how he was best to spend his lonely months in Belgium. Townsend really dislikes personal publicity although there are some who claim that he relishes it. They base this charge on the premise that he courts publicity by his dramatic acts. Even his lone drive round the world has been claimed as a publicity stunt. His troubles perhaps arise from the fact that he never attempts the easy way out of publicity by a half-truth about his actions or movements.

There have been times when I thought he could have been more evasive, even circumspect. But it is against his character not to speak the truth. And this is a family trait. His mother, sisters, and brothers in Somerset must have been hard put to it on many occasions when under extreme pressure from reporters.

When Townsend left London, the exile was to be for only one year. But it quickly became apparent to the Queen, the Queen Mother, and the other members of the royal family, that the Princess was *really* determined to marry Townsend. Margaret then agreed with her sister that he should remain in Brussels until she was twenty-five.

It therefore became even more necessary for Townsend to occupy himself fully. First, he decided to master French. He studied it assiduously for more than a year. Today he speaks it fluently. Townsend has a flare for languages. Second, being fond of riding, he decided to improve his standard and take part in show jumping. He joined the *Étrier Belge*, the most famous riding club in Belgium.

By then he had set up his own home in Brussels. He took a pleasantly furnished £30-a-month apartment at the fashionable end of Avenue Louise. It was rather a small flat with a living room that served as a lounge and dining room, two very small single bedrooms, and a modern kitchen. The furniture was mahogany with blue upholstery, with a close-fitting beige carpet. On the shelf over the fireplace were photographs of his two sons, Giles and Hugo, but none of the Princess. But on his desk in a corner, in a position where no one but the occupant could see it, was a leather folder of snapshots of the Princess. He had had it for several years.

And it was in this flat that he spent most of his leisure hours, reading poetry and the Bible. He once said: "The Bible holds the world's loveliest poetry."

His life was one of simplicity. Often it was thought he held himself unnecessarily aloof from Embassy social life. But he was not really trying to avoid people just because of the romance gossip—but because he prefers a quiet plain way of life. For him that has been the great joy of his journey round the world. And that is why, of all the countries he visited, Africa was the one that impressed him most: the simplicity of the people, their spontaneous gaiety, and a country in which one could be free, if one chose, of mundane life with all its complications.

At the end of a year in Brussels, the standard of Townsend's riding had improved enormously. It was then that he decided to take up racing, and until he finally left Belgium was riding in gentlemen's races two or three times a week. He rode all over Europe—Paris, Madrid, Frankfort, Vienna, Oslo, Milan, and Zurich. In 1955 he had a very successful season. He took his racing as seriously as he has taken everything else in life. Every morning he was up at dawn and rode "work" at the stables of the Belgian trainer, Alfred Hart. He watched his weight and often ran in the woods near his apartment in order to "waste" for a race.

There was one amusing incident in connection with his

Departure.

1958. Princess Margaret on her way to a film premiere after re union with Peter Townsend.

racing, although Townsend did not think so at the time. It happened at Le Tremblay course near Paris.

He rode a horse called Nemrod and passed the winning post fifth. Aly Khan was second. But Townsend, instead of pulling up, went on galloping round the track. Racegoers trained their glasses on the tiny figure in peach and white pounding along the empty track. The horse lapped the course once and still kept going. Twenty minutes after the race ended Townsend came tearing up the straight toward the winning post for the third time. Nemrod was flecked with foam. This time Townsend managed to pull up and dismount. Nemrod had bolted twice before. A reporter dashed up to him and asked: "Why did you keep on galloping?"

"Because I couldn't stop the bloody thing," came the caustic reply.

Early in 1955, Princess Margaret went on a tour of the Caribbean. No doubt many around the Palace hoped that the trip would "get the girl's mind off the business." Margaret enjoyed the holiday, fulfilled her duties impeccably, but was never in danger of forgetting Peter.

When the Princess got back to London, Townsend took a fortnight's leave but remained in Brussels. On the Sunday morning of March 6, the *Sunday Pictorial* in London announced that Princess Margaret is soon "to make this choice: Shall I stay as third in succession to the Throne? Or shall I abdicate my right to succession in order to marry a divorced man, Group Captain Townsend?"

This story was sufficient to fill up Brussels hotels with reporters from all over the world. Townsend, for the first time, found himself besieged in his flat. On Tuesday, having consulted the Princess on the telephone and his Ambassador, Sir Christopher Warner, Townsend decided to break his silence.

He told reporters, when he met them outside his flat: "I am sick of being made to hide in my apartment like a thief."

When asked if he was to marry the Princess, he replied: "I obviously cannot answer this because it involves more people than myself. I came to Brussels because the position was becoming impossible for both of us, especially for her."

Somebody then asked him why he had taken leave just as the rumors were revived. He replied: "I always take leave this time of the year."

It so happened that it was bitterly cold in Brussels early in March that year, with snow on the ground. This did not stop Townsend from getting up as soon as it was light and driving off in his green Renault Fregate to the stables of Alfred Hart. This proved an ordeal for the reporters and photographers, as they could not run the risk of his slipping out of Brussels without their knowledge. So they had to begin their daily vigil before it was even light.

Once Townsend had decided to meet the press he became almost gay. Leaning from the window of his car, he would call to the reporters with a little irony in his voice: "I say, are you trying to get hold of me?" He was like a man released from an invisible leash.

This gaiety, however, was not solely connected with his decision to come out of hiding.

No doubt Townsend, while Margaret was away on her royal tours of the Caribbean, had been a trifle apprehensive. He knew the pressures to which she was being subjected. Could she withstand them?

But his fears evidently proved groundless. The moment the Princess was back in Clarence House she picked up her "green line" telephone and called Townsend in Brussels. The romance still bloomed; she still intended to marry him. That perhaps explained why Townsend suddenly appeared carefree.

In London, of course, there was a flurry. Dignified papers like the *Times* and the government-supervised B.B.C. made no mention of what was on everybody's lips. But the mass-circulation tabloids broke into passionate debate. The *Daily Sketch* cooed over "our little dolly Princess" and in an editorial said: "Every woman will feel deeply for the Princess as she confronts her decision, for whichever way it goes it must be painful." The first reaction in London seemed to be to let the Princess marry whom she wanted to, but the deeply conservative countryside was yet to be heard from.

At the Palace, a careful ear was cocked for the tone of public reaction. The Archbishop of Canterbury talked for three hours over lunch with the Queen and Prince Philip, before Philip went off to fleet maneuvers in the Mediterranean.

Whether the Queen had given up hope of being able to give her consent to the marriage, cannot be known. The Queen was very sympathetic toward her sister. She had seen the Princess' mild flirtations in her late teens but she had also seen the big thing happen—love for the first time, real love. The Queen could not think of her own happy married life without wishing the same for her young sister. Moreover, the Queen knew how lonely and isolated her sister was. It would be churlish to suggest that she would not wish that the burden be lessened, and happily so, for the Princess.

But the Queen's duty was clear. The late Dr. Cosmo Gordon Lang, who was Archbishop of Canterbury at the time of the 1936 crisis, had insisted that the Church could not approve King Edward's proposed marriage to Mrs. Simpson, and the Archbishop, Dr. Geoffrey Fisher, in the spring of 1955 was equally adamant. So was Sir Winston Churchill. He had sturdily defended Edward's wish to marry Mrs. Simpson, but he felt that the Duke of Windsor's semiexile had brought much unhappiness and he did not want to see Princess Margaret go through the same experience.

Through all the hullabaloo, the Princess remained placid and looked radiant. She went twice to the theater with friends and attended a ceremonial "Welcome Home" luncheon given in her honor by the Lord Mayor of London at the Guildhall. Next to her sat the Archbishop. She chatted to him amiably

—but only about her tour. When she left she got a rousing cheer from a waiting crowd. At the weekend she retired for a rest to the Royal Lodge at Windsor with her mother.

All that week in Brussels, Townsend continued to be quizzed by reporters. Then a correspondent for the Sydney *Sun-Herald* reported that Townsend had told him: "If a situation should demand my exile and that of a certain lady, we should, of course, accept it." This interview was a fabrication. Townsend promptly denied he had said anything about exile. Investigating, the *Sun-Herald* agreed that Townsend had been misquoted. The reporter was dismissed.

The incident, however, did serve Townsend one useful purpose. It provided him with an admirable excuse to stop talking to the reporters. Gradually they packed their bags and went home.

In London the guess was that resolute Princess Margaret would end up as the wife of Peter Townsend. But there would be no announcement until the Princess's twenty-fifth birthday in August.

Whether Townsend was wise in permitting himself to be quizzed by reporters is open to argument. True, he could not go on being a prisoner in his own flat. He had to go about his daily life. But the moment he started giving interviews he rendered himself liable to misrepresentation. He should have been given official assistance. It is possible, of course, that both Townsend and the Princess were curious to see what the public reaction would be to the possibility of their marrying. This would have been a fair public relations exercise. Unfortunately for the couple, their cause was championed by the tabloid press who were exploiting the situation merely because of its circulation value. And that section of the press could hardly be expected to be interested in the grave Constitutional issues involved by such a marriage.

It was, therefore, not surprising that the powerful *Daily Mail* on March 15, 1955, should publish a very critical editorial about Townsend's tactics. I quote this editorial in full because it probably represented the thinking at the time of a great many people. The editorial stated:

"Many of our readers will be puzzled and astonished by the statement concerning Princess Margaret made by Group Captain Peter Townsend which appears in the *Daily Mail* this morning.

"It refers to an untrue newspaper report implying that Princess Margaret had decided to marry him. 'The Princess,' he says, 'has made no such decision known to me, nor have I any reason to believe she has made such a decision.'

"It is the matter-of-fact tone of this statement and the calm acceptance of the possibility which will astonish readers who have not already been informed.

"The story began nearly two years ago when an affection was reported between Princess Margaret and a palace equerry, Group Captain Peter Townsend, a man with two children, and an innocent party in a divorce case. When this report was made public he had gone to Brussels as air attaché. There he remains.

"Nine days ago, when the Princess returned from her West Indian tour, the *Sunday Pictorial* revived this old story. They said the royal tour was a 'last gesture' to help the Princess decide whether she should marry the attaché or not.

"At once the world's press converged on Brussels, and the Group Captain began to talk. Here is an assortment of his reported remarks:

" 'Oh, yes, indeed, I know how important it is, but the word cannot come from me.' 'I cannot answer questions about it because I am not a prime mover in this situation.' 'There can be nothing said until the time is ready or somebody does something.'

"These Delphic utterances did nothing to stem the rising flood of interest. Indeed, they did much to encourage it, for they implied that there was 'something in it.'

"Then an Australian paper reported Peter Townsend as saying: 'If a situation should demand my exile and that of a certain lady we should, of course, accept it.' This, he said, was an invention, 'and like a number of similar reported statements should be completely disregarded.'

"But which statements should be dismissed and which accepted we do not know, for he did not say.

"Group Captain Townsend is a man of forty. He cannot be innocent of the ways of the world or of the use which could be made of any ambiguous statements he made about Princess Margaret.

"It seems to us he would have been better advised and served the interests of the Princess and the Royal Family better if he had refused to speak at all.

"It was in the hope that he would be actuated by discretion that the *Daily Mail* declined to take part in the sensational exploitation of this matter. But after the considered statement made by the Group Captain yesterday we feel that a responsible newspaper can no longer ignore it.

"The one sentence in which he refers to the possibility of marriage forces the whole thing from the realm of tattle into that of policy.

"It would be idle to say that Princess Margaret must be allowed to order such a matter in privacy, because obviously the marriage of the Queen's only sister is of high State importance.

"But we can at least hope that the Group Captain has spoken his last word in hurried and unconsidered interviews, and that if there is anything more to be said the Royal Family may be allowed to say it."

This outspoken editorial may now be viewed as completely unfair to Peter Townsend. But if it carried a criticism of Townsend, it also, by implication, was critical of the Palace. I think, that as early as 1953, when Townsend left the Court for Brussels, a considered statement from the Queen's Secretary might have done a great deal to mitigate the unenviable position in which Townsend found himself and at the same time put a stop to newspaper reports which could only be damaging to Princess Margaret and the Crown.

For the rest of the spring and summer, Townsend busied

himself with his office duties, his riding and racing. He now felt confident that his long period of waiting would have a happy ending.

In the summer, there were anonymous letters, threatening Peter's life. They were sent to the Belgian Minister of War. The Belgian police believed that the letters had a political origin. He was immediately given an armed bodyguard by the Belgian military security department. Michel, the guard, carried a Luger pistol in a holster tucked under his armpit. Michel accompanied Peter everywhere—even to the race meetings. Outside the Avenue Louise apartment there was a day-and-night guard of uniformed policemen. All strangers trying to enter the apartment building were scrutinized.

By the middle of August, editors in Fleet Street and else-where throughout the world were beginning to prepare their readers for Sunday, August 21—the day that Princess Margaret would celebrate her twenty-fifth birthday. The significance of the day, as I have already stated, was that at twenty-five the Princess would no longer have to seek her sister's permission to marry. But everybody seemed to ignore the fact that though free at twenty-five, Margaret, as an heir to the throne, still had to reckon with objections from Parliament, where the Bishops and the High Anglican peers in the House of Lords and the powerful nonconformist back-benchers in the House of Commons could make trouble. The question was: Could Margaret trade her right of succession to the throne for marriage with the man of her choice?

The lurid tabloids were headlining August 21 as the day "she can marry whom she pleases."

All that Buckingham Palace would say about the Princess' birthday was that there would be a quiet royal family picnic beside Scotland's granite, ivy-covered, many-turreted Balmoral Castle. "Ruby" (Robina MacDonald, her personal maid) would tiptoe upstairs and waken the Princess with a cup of tea and her first Happy Birthday. Then there would be prayers, breakfast of grilled herrings, the usual reading of the Sunday newspapers with her mother, after which the whole family would gather in the green drawing room for the opening of birthday presents, arriving at the Castle in sealed red mailbags. The party would then attend service at the parish church of Crathie.

Of course what the reporters roaming the Deeside moors hoped was that Peter Townsend would make a dramatic appearance at the Castle.

In Brussels hotels were again filling up with journalists, radio commentators, and cameramen from all over the world.

On Wednesday evening Townsend slipped out of Brussels in his official black Vanguard saloon to a country retreat. At the British Embassy it was stated he had gone on leave for a fortnight. This act unleashed another flood of rumors. The truth was that Peter was giving his sons, Giles and Hugo, a holiday.

Then on Saturday he turned up in Ostend. Before a crowd of 15,000 people he won in a photo finish the third race on a five-year-old mare named Kwenda. The odds 11–4. His colors: Red cap, white shirt.

Peter got off to a rather bad start but gradually edged forward until, using the whip, he drew level with the favorite, Armagnac, in the straight. People in the grandstand rose to their feet and shouted in English: "Come on, Townsend." After the finish admirers scrambled through the fences and ran up to congratulate him.

The next day, the Princess' birthday, Peter was riding again at Ostend races. During the afternoon he was called from the race track to go to the British Consulate to take a telephone call. He explained afterward that it was only to receive a telegram, asking him to ride a horse.

From Ostend, Peter took his sons on to Deauville, where he was again riding and from there to Oslo for another race. He landed in the middle of the racecourse by helicopter. An hour later he rode the winner. By now, of course, owners were anxious for him to ride their horses. At the racecourses of

France, Germany, Sweden, Italy, and Spain he was a "draw." Shyly he responded to the acclaim of thousands of people who accepted without reservation that the romance between him and Princess Margaret was a fact.

Early in September, Townsend flew to London for the European Air Attachés conference at the Air Ministry and the Farnborough Air Show. This time he did not see Princess Margaret who was still at Balmoral. But there must have been a good many telephone conversations, the couple making arrangements for their meeting later in October when Peter was to take leave.

On Saturday, October 1, the Prime Minister, now Sir Anthony Eden, flew north with Lady Eden to be guests of the Queen for the weekend at Balmoral. It was intended that Sir Anthony should make this visit earlier but at the last minute he had had to cancel the arrangements because of ill health.

The visit of Sir Anthony to Balmoral was important. The Queen now knew that her sister had definitely decided to marry Townsend. Although there had been many informal discussions two years earlier, when Sir Winston Churchill was Premier, this meeting with Sir Anthony was the first formal discussion.

The Queen discussed the problem on Saturday evening alone with Sir Anthony before dinner and after dinner the Prime Minister talked with Princess Margaret.

Sir Anthony made the position of his Cabinet quite clear. It was correct that under the Royal Marriages Act, Princess Margaret, now twenty-five, merely had to give notice in writing to the Privy Council of her intention to marry Group Captain Townsend and if Parliament did not object within one year, the wedding could take place. But if the Princess wished to retain her royal status, then the marriage would be opposed by the Government and resolutions would be tabled in both Houses of Parliament. The Prime Minister recognized that the Government resolutions might not be carried, but he was confident that they would be. Even if there were defections in his own party, many Socialist M.P.'s might support the Government's action. Further, the Government's views were supported by the Commonwealth Governments.

What was the alternative?

Lawyers had worked out that if the Princess abdicated her rights of succession to the throne, Parliament would virtually forfeit its right to object, since it would be objecting to the marriage of a private person.

For this there was a valuable precedent in the abdication of Margaret's uncle. Between 11.19 and 11.23 on the evening of December 11, 1936, the Prime Minister, Mr. Stanley Baldwin, after announcing the King's intention to abdicate, added, "It would clearly be wrong that the provisions of the Royal Marriages Act should apply to His Majesty and his descendants who, on the passing of this [Abdication] Act, will cease to have any right in the succession."

Therefore, if the Princess was to marry Group Captain Townsend, said Sir Anthony, it would be necessary to ask Parliament to pass a bill, the terms of which would:

> Deprive Princess Margaret and her issue of all rights of succession to the throne.
>
> Deprive her of her right to function as a Counsellor of State, which she with others of the royal family, exercise when the sovereign is incapacitated or during a long absence from the country.
>
> Deprive her of the £6,000 which she receives under the Civil List, and £15,000 a year which she would receive on marriage.

Nor did the Prime Minister think it practical that Princess Margaret and her husband should live in England for a time after their marriage. He did not suggest, however, that the couple should be permanently exiled, as has virtually happened in the case of the Windsors.

From political sources at the time I was informed that this

was not all that Sir Anthony had to say to both the Queen and the Princess. Whichever course were chosen, he felt it his duty to state that some irreparable damage would be done to the standing of royalty. In this he had the full support of the Marquess of Salisbury, the Lord President of the Council, and the Leader of the House of Lords.

Further, Lord Salisbury had hinted to the Prime Minister that if the Princess decided she wished to marry Group Captain Townsend and a Bill of Renunciation (as it was likely to be called) were necessary, then he might feel compelled to resign from the Government. If he did not resign, he, as Leader of the House of Lords, would be responsible for the passage of the bill through that House. Lord Salisbury, as a High Anglican, felt that if Parliament passed such a bill it would be condoning action which the Queen, as head of the Established Church could not approve, and which the Church itself could not accept. This argument was consistent with Salisbury's high principles—principles with which many persons find themselves in full sympathy.

This news must have been a shock to both the Queen and the Princess. Century after century, Lord Salisbury's family, the Cecils, have served their King and their country. It was to Salisbury that the Queen turned for advice when she had to choose between Mr. Macmillan and Mr. Butler to form a government after Eden's resignation following the Suez crisis.

So no contemporary history is complete without looking closely at the Cecil family as we did at the Battenbergs.

By birth and marriage, Lord Salisbury is related to half the noble families in Britain. It is said that "a Cecil never smiles except when another Cecil enters the room."

With his bony face and mild Edwardian lisp, Salisbury at first meeting may look like a slightly astringent edition of a P. G. Wodehouse hero. But behind the prim manner and pained eyebrows lurks a will as strong as Churchill's. An admirer some years ago said to me: "Bobbety has the same political acumen as Herbert Morrison [then the most powerful figure in the Socialist Party] but with this difference: the Marquess has been at the game 450 years longer."

Fifteenth-century records list the Cecils as "municipal worthies" in the Lincolnshire city of Stamford. They were ancient and loyal vassals of the Tudor Kings, and when Henry VIII confiscated the lands of the Roman Church, the Cecils got their share.

William Cecil, first Baron Burghley, served Elizabeth I as Chief Adviser and Lord High Treasurer. It was he who sent Mary Queen of Scots to the block. His son, Robert, brought the Stuart dynasty to England in 1603, lived to hear King James I dub him his "little beagle."

By serving their country and their monarchs through the centuries the Cecils earned a rich reward. In Queen Victoria's day, Robert, the third Marquess, was three times Tory Prime Minister. It was he, "Bobbety's" grandfather, who drove Winston Churchill's father out of his Cabinet and out of public life.

The historian Thomas Macaulay wrote a harsh judgment on the founder of the Cecil family: "Of the willow and not of the oak." But it could be said with truth of the present Marquess of Salisbury that he is of the willow, pliable when he was leading the House of Lords, but also of the oak when a principle is involved.

He was elected to Parliament in 1927 and in the House of Commons joined forces with the fast-rising star in the Conservative Party, fellow Etonian Anthony Eden. He became Eden's deputy at the Foreign Office. When Chamberlain decided to "appease" Mussolini, it was Salisbury who urged Eden to resign as a protest. When he did, Salisbury followed.

Perhaps it was Eden's finest hour, but with his eye on the future he pledged his loyalty to the Conservative Party. Salisbury, as a Cecil, felt no need to protest his party loyalty. He bluntly told the Commons that Chamberlain's policy was "surrender to blackmail." After Munich and Chamberlain's promise of "Peace with honor," Salisbury demanded, "Where is honor?" The right policy, he said, was "rearm, rearm, and rearm."

Eden and Salisbury—the "Foreign Office Twins"—were called back to office in Winston Churchill's wartime coalition. Churchill and Salisbury frequently disagreed. Salisbury alone could silence Churchill.

It is perhaps significant that when the Margaret-Townsend affair began in 1953, Eden was ill and so was Churchill. Butler was acting Prime Minister but Salisbury was the real power in the Government. Before his illness, Churchill had proposed a meeting at the Summit. Salisbury was bitterly opposed. He persuaded Butler to put him temporarily in charge of the Foreign Office. He went to Washington and, allying himself with Dulles, killed Churchill's idea.

The Cecil family motto is: *"Sero sed Serio"*—"Late, but Seriously"—another way of likening the Cecils to the tortoise in its race with the hare.

So it is not surprising if on that Sunday morning after learning of Lord Salisbury's opposition, there was a serious expression on Margaret's face as she drove with the rest of the royal family to Crathie Church for morning service.

Hundreds of people were waiting outside to see her. They believed a vital decision had just been made in regard to her future. In the Church she sat with bowed head. When she came out she smiled uncertainly at the sympathetic crowd, then looked quickly away.

That afternoon Townsend was riding in Milan. He finished next to last.

No doubt Eden made the most of Salisbury's attitude. And knowing Salisbury, he could not ignore the threat of resignation. When Salisbury resigned from the Chamberlain Government he said: "My resignation is a matter of fundamental principle. . . . It is a principle of good faith in international affairs." If Salisbury felt that a matter of principle was involved in asking Parliament to provide a way for the Princess to marry a divorced commoner, then Eden knew that Salisbury would not hesitate to do so. Could Eden afford to run such a grave risk to his newly-elected government?

Yet once Princess Margaret got over her initial shock at the combined attitude of Eden and Salisbury, she showed even more determination than ever to marry Townsend. The Princess is a person of great courage. Today her husband would be Peter Townsend but for one factor which the Princess, as she walked the Deeside hills in those autumn days of 1955, did not visualize.

# The Crisis

ON WEDNESDAY, OCTOBER 12, 1955, THE GAYEST PRINCESS MARgaret that Scotland had seen all the summer stepped from her car at Aberdeen station. She was smiling and radiant in a biscuit-colored suit with a pleated skirt and a tight-fitting off-the-face hat of slate gray. She wore a double string of pearls and a lapel ornament.

With the Princess were Princess Alexandra, Lady Elizabeth Cavendish, and Lady Rose Baring.

In the corridor of one of the four royal coaches that were attached to the Perth train, the Princess laughed gaily with Princess Alexandra, and waved to a small crowd.

It was said that the Princess was leaving Balmoral five days earlier than planned. These statements were based on the fact that the Queen, Prince Charles, and Princess Anne were not to travel to London until Sunday night. Prince Philip was in Denmark on a five days' visit.

There was nothing accidental about all these arrangements, including Princess Alexandra's traveling with Margaret. The Duchess of Kent had sympathy for Margaret and Peter.

The Queen Mother had been spending a few days at home, Castle Mey in Caithness. But she was to leave Wick by air in a Royal Viking for London the next morning.

Also on October 12, across the Channel, Group Captain Townsend—the man who would not say Yes and who would not say No—was leaving Brussels. All the way from Brussels to Le Touquet, to Lydd, and then on to London, he brushed aside questions. From the Sussex airport to London he was followed by a cavalcade of Press cars and photographers on motorcycles.

175

On the flight across the Channel he sat with the pilot, Captain Douglas Phillips. When the other half dozen passengers left by the fuselage, Townsend appeared in the nose of the aircraft as the cargo doors swung open. He walked down the loading ramp and shook hands with the airport manager. To reporters, all he would say was: "I shall stay here three or four weeks. I know nothing about any announcement."

From Lydd he drove straight to the London flat of the Marquess of Abergavenny in Lowndes Square off Knightsbridge. He unloaded his luggage and parked his car across the road by the gardens.

This flat is used mostly by Lord Rupert Nevill, the Marquess' brother. Lord Rupert, a friend of the royal family and of Townsend, had been at Balmoral Castle a few days earlier to make all the arrangements for looking after Peter during his stay in London. At the time it was not generally known that Townsend was a godfather of Lord Rupert's daughter, Angela.

Other friends of the royal family had also been alerted, as well as personal friends of Princess Margaret, to provide the couple with hospitality while they reached their difficult final decision.

But at that moment there was not much doubt about the answer. Townsend had a confident smile when he arrived at Lowndes Square. The next morning the Princess looked wonderfully happy as she left Euston Station and drove to Clarence House.

This, however, was only the beginning of nineteen days of tension—nineteen days of near-crisis. What had begun as a simple and sentimental story of a princess in love was to become a crisis that deeply involved institutions close to the heart of every Englishman: the Crown and the Established Church. In the beginning it seemed that almost everyone was on the side of romance. Margaret, the nation's royal darling, should be allowed to marry the man she loves, people were saying. It did not seem to matter that her choice, the airman who had been her father's Equerry, was a commoner; it mattered only a little that at forty-one he was sixteen years older than she: it would matter only to some that he was a divorced man with two sons.

That was how it began and the news seeped slowly upward from the least respectable and least responsible newspapers. With no other way of knowing what was going on, the people who habitually read only the *Times* and listened to the B.B.C. would not even have guessed at the romance when Townsend arrived back from Brussels and the Princess came down from her native Scotland.

And this was a deceptive atmosphere for both Townsend and the Princess, who were completely without experienced, independent advisers. Their situation was no better than that in which King Edward VIII found himself in 1936. Those who tried to advise him then did not really know the true sense of public opinion. Nor did the Princess and her airman suitor now.

On that October morning, a few hours before they were to have their first meeting at Clarence House, the way no doubt seemed not too difficult for them, although they knew that the terms of their marriage were onerous.

Everywhere Townsend went on that pleasant, crisp Thursday, October 13, he was treated as a celebrity. Shortly before one o'clock Mrs. John Lycett Wills, first cousin of the Queen and Princess Margaret, arrived at Lowndes Square to lunch with Townsend. Mrs. Wills's mother, Lady Elphinstone, is a sister of the Queen Mother and Mrs. Wills had known the Queen and the Princess since childhood. They were at her wedding twenty years previously. The Princess is a godmother to the seven-year-old Marilyn, one of Mrs. Wills's three children. And Marilyn was a playmate of Prince Charles and Princess Anne.

After lunch, Townsend, smiling and confident, went on a hundred-minute shopping tour in the West End. Mrs. Wills drove him in her green Morris Oxford. As he came down the steps of the Lowndes Square block of flats, he put his hands on the bonnet of the car and said to the reporters: "Well, what are you all waiting for?" Through the hubbub of questions about Princess Margaret, he replied: "I'm just going shopping. I shall be back in half an hour." And then a little desperately when pressed, "You'll just have to wait and see what I'm doing tonight."

From Lowndes Square Mrs. Wills drove him to the late King's tailor in Bury Street to order a suit. Police had waived the no parking rules and more police held up the traffic in crowded Jermyn Street so that Mrs. Wills could drive Townsend to another tailor in Conduit Street for a pair of breeches. The last shop was a cake shop in Sloane Street. She came out with two boxes of fancy cakes, which she handed to Townsend who held them on his knees. Back at Lowndes Square, Townsend ran the gantlet of reporters and photographers, waving cheerily to Mrs. Wills as she drove away.

At six twenty he came down the steps and walked across the road to his green Renault Fregate. He was hatless, as usual, and had changed his tweed suit for a double-breasted dark-gray lounge suit and pearl tie. Nervously he fumbled with the door keys of his car as he told reporters once more: "You'll have to wait and see."

He drove straight to Clarence House, parking his car in Ambassadors Court. He walked across to a small door marked "Household Officers." For a moment he paused uncertainly. "Is this the door or is it the next one?" he asked aloud. "They've altered things a bit. No, it must be this one."

At a touch of the bell the door was opened by a young man in a dark suit. For a moment they chatted and then the door closed.

Only half an hour earlier the Queen Mother had driven through the main gates after landing at London Airport by air from Scotland.

The Queen Mother was not present at this meeting.

It would be appropriate to indicate at this point the attitude of the Queen Mother toward the proposed marriage. She was against it and she used the argument with her daughter that her father, the late King, would have opposed such a marriage. It was painful to the Queen Mother to take this attitude. She had always been fond of Townsend and she knew her late husband's feelings toward the young Equerry. But she also knew where her daughter's duty lay. She was more rigid in her attitude than the Queen. The latter would do her duty—and did it—but if Margaret had decided to marry Townsend, the elder sister would not have indulged in recriminations. She would have wished her sister lifelong happiness.

It was eight ten P.M. before Townsend left Clarence House after this first meeting. They had been together two hours. He came out the same back door—but it was the last time he was to use the servants' entrance. Ever afterward he either used the garden entrance through St. James's Palace or drove in through the main gates. Townsend was now a suitor for the Princess' hand in marriage.

As he walked across Ambassadors Court to his car he was surrounded by reporters. To them he said: "I am sorry but I can't say anything. I am going back to Lowndes Square where I shall turn in early. I'm feeling pretty tired." As hundreds of flash bulbs went off in his face, he joked: "I only hope I'm not too blinded to drive."

Back at Lowndes Square he was again besieged by dozens of reporters. One said: "You don't know what a state the newspapers are in about this." Townsend quipped: "You don't know what a state I'm in." It was an accurate statement.

As Townsend went to bed, the headlines in the New York newspapers read: "Meg arrives. Verdict soon."—*Daily News*. "London agog as Margaret trails Captain."—*World Telegram*. "Meg home and all ask: 'Is it yes?'"—*Journal American*. "Meg and Peter in London . . . and now?"—New York *Post*. Two years previously these same newspapers had been

castigated by some sections of the London press for talking
about the Margaret-Townsend romance. Now they were vin-
dicated and getting their own back.

But if the British press had played down the story hitherto,
the Clarence House meeting opened the floodgates.

The *Daily Mail* which only a few months earlier had been
very harsh toward Townsend, now said:

> ". . . When Princess Margaret returned to London from Scot-
> land she had never looked happier or more lovely. She was
> radiant. Her photographs could have been those of a girl
> whose engagement to marry had at last been put beyond
> question. Nor did the pictures of the Group Captain show
> one who was any less joyful. His was not the demeanour of
> a man worried by false reports, or strained by the unaccus-
> tomed limelight. He appeared to be relaxed and 'on top of
> the world.'
>
> ". . . Group Captain Townsend has that claim upon our
> consideration which must always belong to The Few. He was
> one of the fighter pilots who won the Battle of Britain, and
> even in that select company he gained distinction for cour-
> age.
>
> "He was highly thought of by King George VI, to whom he
> was an Equerry. This is something of which any man can be
> proud, for that good sovereign was no mean judge of char-
> acter.
>
> ". . . Group Captain Townsend was the innocent party in a
> divorce action. The British people could have wished that
> such complications could have been absent. But if the Prin-
> cess has made her choice it only remains for them to wish
> her long life and every happiness. . . . The British people
> would welcome it for the sake of a beloved Princess."

And that opinion set the tone of the popular newspapers.
The staid press held its fire.

On Friday afternoon the Princess and the Group Captain
left London to spend the weekend in the country at Allanbay
Park, the twenty-room home in Berkshire of Major and Mrs.
Wills. As soon as the Princess left London, a statement was

issued from Clarence House in an attempt to damp down newspaper speculation. The initiative for the communiqué came from Commander Richard Colville, the Queen's Press Secretary. If he really thought that such a procedure was going to discourage the world's newspapers from writing about this royal romance, then his knowledge of public relations must have been very limited. No doubt he knew it was a vain hope but thought it might do something toward securing a calmer atmosphere in which the final decision would be taken. Commander Colville and other officials at the Court were against the marriage. It was, therefore, in their interests (one might almost say vested interests) to delay the decision sufficiently long until public opinion began to veer the other way. In a sense, their tactics succeeded.

The statement, issued on Friday evening, said:

> "In view of the varied reports which have been published, the Press Secretary to the Queen is authorised to say that no announcement concerning Princess Margaret's personal future is at present contemplated.
>
> "The Princess has asked the Press Secretary to express the hope that the Press and public will extend to her Royal Highness their customary courtesy and co-operation in respecting her privacy."

The interpretation which political commentators put on this announcement was that only official formalities had to be completed for the betrothal to be announced.

So that weekend world attention was focused on a sleepy Berkshire village with its scattered farmhouses and quaint old English inn.

The royal drama came to Binfield at three fifty-five P.M. on Friday, October 14, when the sleek green Renault Fregate (now the most photographed car in London) swung off the Twyford road into the tree-lined drive of Allanbay Park. At the wheel was Townsend, smiling but looking a trifle strained. Two and a half hours later the Princess' Rolls

Royce did not slow down as it approached the green gates of
Allanbay, but traveled at thirty miles an hour as it entered
the driveway. It flew no standard. The windows were cur-
tained, although the Princess could be seen clutching the
handrest to steady herself. She blinked in a blaze of photographers' flashlights. As the car disappeared down the drive,
police escorts moved in swiftly. A patrol car blocked the entrance to the drive. The six-foot-high spiked gates were
slammed shut. From his own car in the shadows, the Chief
Constable of Berkshire, Mr. J. W. Waldron, directed the security cordon which was flung around the fifty-acre wooded
estate. The square Georgian house, covered with Virginia
creeper, could not be seen from the road. Inside the wall
surrounding the estate a police dog and its handler patrolled
through shrubbery bordering the lawn. Outside other police
dog teams circled the walls. Six police cars patrolled slowly
around the surrounding roads. Inside the closed gates were
two policemen. At vantage points around the long boundary
of the estate were police with walkie-talkie radio sets, and
radio-equipped motorcyclists were in constant touch with the
command car at the park gates.

Looking back on these elaborate security precautions one
might be forgiven for thinking that they had been taken to
protect the lives of world statesmen meeting in a neutral
country. In fact, all that was really happening was that a
young couple deeply in love were being given a chance to
decide whether they wished to marry in the face of family,
church, and political opposition. Why did they suddenly
need this protection? Had they not spent hours together
roaming the Scottish moors a few years earlier? Did propriety
now demand in the middle of the twentieth century that
Victorian conventions be adhered to? From whom were the
young couple being protected? Presumably the newspapers.

No doubt I shall be accused of having a vulgar attitude toward publicity about royalty. But if the Princess and her airman suitor had been just an ordinary woman and man in

love, they would have been given by their parents every opportunity to settle their problem alone and in freedom. The simple solution is usually the most satisfactory.

Nor can the press be blamed for vulgar curiosity. Princess Margaret belonged to the nation. Much of the newspaper sordidness of that weekend at Allanbay and the final weekend at Uckfield in Sussex could have been avoided if someone had been made responsible for insuring that the newspaper reporters and cameramen were given some assistance. Here the Palace erred. There was no reason why Princess Margaret and Group Captain Townsend should not have been photographed together. There was no reason why a responsible official of the Palace should not have explained to the newspapers something of the current situation. Everybody, of course, knew the difficulties and the dilemma in which Margaret and Peter found themselves. And, in truth, everybody was sympathetic. It was too naïve to expect silence just because a request had been made for privacy.

The *Manchester Guardian* made this outspoken comment on the morning after the communiqué requesting privacy:

> ". . . Whether it will have much effect is another matter . . . whatever our distaste for sensationalism and emotionalism we have also to recognise that in the affairs of the Queen's sister we touch matters of State—and Church—that are of public concern."

The editorial then pointed out that the months of discussion had brought out that the mass of the people believed "firmly that the Princess should marry whom she wants, whether noble or commoner, single man or divorcé, *so long as he is a British Protestant.*"

The *Guardian* then claimed there was "growing impatience with obsolete forms like the Royal Marriages Act and the technicalities a spiteful king introduced to hurt his family a hundred and eighty years ago." The provisions of the Act were described as "nonsense."

". . . To invoke any of this mumbo-jumbo now would be ridiculous. Better repeal the Act straight away as a matter of grace and fair play."

Dealing with the question of the renunciation of succession by the Princess, the *Guardian* asked:

"Why should this be so? Her accession is a very remote chance with a young Sovereign and two young children ahead of her. And even if it were not remote, would the idea of a non-royal consort be so terrible if our democracy means anything?

"There remains the question of the attitude of the Church of England, or rather a section of the Church of England, and of the Roman Catholic Church to marriage with the innocent party of a divorce. On that there is only one thing to be said. If we can have a Prime Minister, Cabinet ministers, judges, who are 'innocent parties' we can, without feeling unduly disturbed in our moral fibre, give the same latitude to the Queen's sister. And if there is any difficulty about marriage by the officers of the State Church, English Nonconformity and the Church of Scotland, no less representative of the people of Britain will be willing to do their part."

Too much blame must not be put on enterprising photographers who climbed trees and crept through the undergrowth with telephoto lenses to secure photographs of the Princess and Townsend walking in the beautiful wooded grounds of Allanbay or beside the lake. It was quite wrong, of course, for one French magazine to offer the butler £1,000 for "inside" information. It is to the credit of the butler that he refused.

But the press did have a *liaison* with someone inside the house. Little fair-haired Marilyn Wills from time to time on that Saturday morning walked down to the main gate and disseminated tidbits of news. However, this hole in the security curtain was speedily plugged when the family discovered what was happening. If her behind-the-scenes news had any veracity, then the romance was going along very nicely. Marilyn, however, did seem to be drawing on her imagination to satisfy the news-hungry reporters. Nevertheless, she did achieve one distinction: Marilyn was the only person ever to give a first-person quoted interview on the affair.

Saturday at Allanbay Park was no doubt spent like any other day at a weekend country house party. Townsend rode before breakfast on a horse from the nearby stables of Miss Norah Wilmot. During the morning the Princess in tweeds and Townsend wearing a gray sweater strolled in the gardens where the Queen and Philip had walked and had picnics before their marriage. After a while the couple returned to the house and a few minutes later came out again, Peter now wearing a jacket. They walked through the rose garden to the lake. After dinner, Margaret played the piano. Peter lounged in an armchair.

On this day there was not very much serious talk between them. Margaret had really made up her mind. Now she was content to spend her first full day with Townsend for several years.

The next day, Sunday, the Princess drove with Mrs. Wills to the Royal Chapel at Windsor Castle, for the morning service. Townsend stayed behind but did run to a corner of the drive to wave them good-by. Margaret, who was wearing a checked tweed suit with a velvet collar, seemed in a gay mood and peeped through the rear window of the car to see if they were being followed. After the service she chatted for more than half an hour with the Queen Mother. On the return journey to Allanbay, the Princess seemed in a thoughtful mood. Had her mother said something to upset her? Although the Princess had decided to marry Townsend, there is no doubt that emotionally she was still torn between her love for the man and her devotion to the Church. The Princess, an avid reader of newspapers, must have pondered the words written in the solid *Sunday Times* that morning. The editorial read: ". . . The Princess's marriage could lead to a controversy capable of splitting Church and State more profoundly than anything for 300 years."

That evening after dinner, I think that the Princess and Townsend must have begun to consider their position seriously. Could they go through with the marriage in the face of family, church, and political opposition? Doubts must have crept into both their minds. But the decision must rest with the Princess. If she wished marriage—as she had repeatedly said she did over a period of two years—then he would be a very happy man. Was their love, however, strong enough to overcome all obstacles?

When they went to their rooms to bed that night the position was unchanged. The marriage was still on.

In the previous year, the Princess' duties were less arduous than they once were, but she performed them all with conscientious care, managing always to look alert and interested during the windiest dignitary's speech, making her own speeches short and dignified, and flashing her warm smile discreetly where it was most needed. Perhaps her greatest freedom was shopping alone with her lady-in-waiting in London's smartest shops. This pleasure, like others in the grown-up Princess' life, required money that only a Princess could afford.

In setting her heart on Peter Townsend, she had given no indication that she wanted to give up the privileges, duties, or emoluments of the royal life. This prompts the question: Did she still believe that she could have her royal cake and eat it too?

On Monday, October 17, all was peace again at Allanbay and in the village of Binfield. The Princess and Townsend, in separate cars, returned to London. The reporters and the cameramen went with them.

The plea of the Princess, through Commander Colville, for privacy had fallen on deaf ears. Said the *Manchester Guardian* on Monday morning:

"Whether or not Princess Margaret marries, or whoever she decides to marry, her private affairs have certainly attracted an enormous amount of attention. Rightly or wrongly? That depends on acceptance of the theory that the Royal Family is also in some mysterious way a private family. It might be as well if it were, *but the operations of the Buckingham Palace public relations experts make it hardly possible. Such emphasis is put on the public duties and appearances of royalty, so much fervour whipped up, that it is asking too much to expect that the Queen and those close to her should be treated as though they were 'ordinary' people. . . ."*

On the same day the Junior Common Room at Balliol College, Oxford, banned newspapers which "are making the private life of Princess Margaret headline news."

Commented the *Daily Mail* cynically the next day: "They must have virtually cut themselves off from the world's Press."

The only newspapers excluded from the boycott were the *Times,* the *Manchester Guardian,* the *Sunday Times,* and the *Observer.* Quipped the *Mail:* ". . . In *The Times:* 'Princess Margaret at Church.' What right has 'The Times' to pursue her to the pew? . . . To say that the possible marriage of the Queen's sister is nobody else's affair but her own is utter nonsense. It is not even true of any marriage—hence the calling of banns."

From Monday there began a series of private dinner parties with the Princess and Townsend as guests of intimate friends of Margaret. The hostess and host were in each case a little unusual, but not more so than this method of courtship which someone in the royal family had devised. Townsend was either drinking sherry alone with the Princess at Clarence House or eating with her in other people's houses. Why should he not have been invited to dinner at Clarence House by the Queen Mother? One cannot help asking: How could two persons faced with such a dilemma reach a sane decision in such an atmosphere and under such conditions? One can

almost feel embarrassed for their dinner hosts discreetly re-
tiring from the drawing room to give the lovers half an hour
to themselves. At the time, an American journalist friend
asked me: "How do you court a British princess?" And then
added: "Does she ever get a chance to throw her arms round
her suitor and give him a kiss without prying eyes?"

I agreed it was a little difficult to visualize such an outburst
of affection under the prevailing conditions. There was, however, in the case of Princess Margaret and Townsend a difference between their romance and the romances of all other
members of the royal family. They fell in love because they
had in the past every opportunity to do so. They had spent
many hours, even days together, alone. They understood
each other thoroughly—their whims, their idiosyncrasies,
their mutual interests such as theology, music, and literature.
Perhaps basically Margaret is gayer than Peter Townsend.
There is something of the ascetic in his make-up and this
is not a pose. I think that all his life he has been searching
for the truth. Alone he can be a fascinating talker and re-
veals astonishing depths of thought. These unusual qualities,
plus his great charm with women whom he understands, no
doubt appealed to the Princess. He stood head-and-shoulders
higher than all the other men she had met. Therefore, it
was not surprising that she fell in love with him. In fact, it
would have been surprising if she had not.

On Monday evening the Princess and Townsend dined
with the Mark Bonham Carters in Victoria Road, Kensington. Bonham Carter at one time had been talked about as
a suitor of Margaret's. He had been a theater escort and a
party companion.

The choice of the Bonham Carters' home for the first of
the dinner parties was a little surprising. In July Bonham
Carter had married Lady St. Just, the divorced wife of Lord
St. Just. Princess Margaret could not attend the wedding,
but in this hour of need the Princess turned to her old friend
for help and perhaps advice.

Townsend arrived for the dinner party fifteen minutes before the Princess. As she stepped from her Rolls Royce and walked up the garden path, Bonham Carter opened the front door and ran down the steps to greet her. He bowed, shook her by the hand, and then escorted her into the small hallway. Before the door was closed the Princess could be seen climbing the staircase to the dining room on the first floor. She was wearing a black dress with ballet-length skirt of net and a mink wrap about her shoulders. A bracelet of diamonds glittered on her left wrist.

While the dinner was in progress a Black Maria brought a police guard. The Princess' personal "shadow," Inspector Fred Crocker, stood in the hall while two plainclothes policemen paced the small garden. Six uniformed policemen patrolled the roadway.

At ten minutes after midnight the Princess left alone. Twenty-five minutes later Townsend drove back to Lowndes Square.

Tuesday, October 18, was a key day in the crisis. The Queen had returned to Buckingham Palace from Balmoral. In the afternoon the Cabinet met for two hours. Salisbury, who had been to Balmoral in August for a Privy Council meeting, was present.

It would not be true to say that the Cabinet formally discussed the Princess' desire to marry Townsend but there was a lengthy informal talk among the ministers without the presence of the Secretary of the Cabinet and without the taking of minutes.

That evening Sir Anthony Eden, the Prime Minister, was to see the Queen. It was therefore essential that he should know the views of his ministers. The Cabinet was *against* the marriage, but if the Princess insisted on going through with it, there would have to be conditions.

The Princess, however, had a champion for her independence in Beaverbrook's *Daily Express*.

Under the headline: "The Princess's Right," that newspaper stated:

> "It would remain deplorable that her sister [the Queen's sister] should be required to write herself out of the succession.
>
> "A marriage 'on condition' would suggest a marriage not entirely acceptable. The implication would be that the marriage though within the letter of the law had something wrong about it.
>
> "The mass of the British people would utterly regret this. In the public mind, there is no such thing as a 'second class' marriage. Nor is there in morals or in law.
>
> "Princess Margaret will, of course, be anxious to ease the problems of her sister, the Queen. She may therefore be attracted to renunciation of her Royal succession.
>
> "This act of self-denial would do her credit. Just the same it would be mistaken. . . .
>
> "There is no desire to impose any penalty whatever on the Princess for contracting a marriage with Group Captain Townsend. The only reluctance to welcome the match at all comes from a section of ecclesiastical opinion. . . .
>
> "In the minds of millions of Britons rigid in their morality, the Princess's marriage in those circumstances would carry no moral stigma.
>
> "There would be only admiration for her courage and good sense in discounting ecclesiastical arguments that no longer carry authority because they no longer carry conviction.
>
> "Her marriage would be an occasion for nothing but rejoicing and good wishes for her future happiness."

But those sentiments hardly represented the views of the Cabinet on that Tuesday afternoon. Nearer the truth was what the distinguished London correspondent of the New York *Times*, Mr. Drew Middleton, close friend of Eden, cabled to his newspaper: "The crux of the matter is not whether Margaret should marry Townsend—there does not seem to be much public opposition to that—but how the marriage is to be accomplished without jolting the delicate relationship of the Crown, Church and Government that stands at the apex of British authority."

In that sentence lay the strength of Salisbury's arguments: Could the government be a willing party to something which the Queen, as Defender of the Faith, could not sanction? Moreover, Salisbury was also able to point out that the Commonwealth countries would disapprove of the marriage unless Margaret gave up her royal titles and yet would agree with great reluctance to her surrendering her right of succession. Any act which the British Parliament made law to ease the way for the marriage would require also the approval, under the terms of the Statute of Westminster, of all the Commonwealth Parliaments.

At this meeting of Ministers Salisbury did not again threaten to resign if he were called upon to sponsor an enabling bill in the Lords, but Eden knew that the Lord President of the Council might in the end do so and, in consequence, undermine the position of the government.

While all this argument was going on at 10 Downing Street, Townsend was driving his green Renault through the iron-studded black gates of Clarence House. It was his second visit. This time he was using the entrance reserved for members of the royal family.

It was four ten when he went in. Five minutes later the Queen Mother went out but came back in half an hour.

Townsend stayed for two hours. A few minutes after he left, the Princess, gay and smiling, drove to Claridge's Hotel for a reception in her honor by the Royal Air Force Cinema Corporation. It was her first official engagement after her summer holiday. Wearing an emerald silk cocktail dress with gathered neckline and sleeves, she was greeted by the Air Minister, Lord De L'Isle and Dudley. They chatted to film chiefs and while talking to Air Chief Marshal Sir Francis Fogarty the Princess sipped a champagne cocktail and smoked a cigarette in a long black holder.

While Margaret was at Claridge's, Eden had driven across from Downing Street to Buckingham Palace for an audience with the Queen. The Prime Minister in a ninety-minute talk informed the Queen of his Cabinet's views and stressed the attitude of Salisbury. No doubt it was convenient to Eden, a divorced man who had married again—the second time to Clarissa Churchill, a niece of Winston Churchill—to use Salisbury as the spearhead of attack.

Eden then put the terms of marriage if Princess Margaret refused to withdraw. These terms were identical to those which he had less formally put to the Queen and the Princess at Balmoral earlier in the month: renunciation of her place as third in line to the succession and retirement to private life. And that carried with it forfeiture of her income under the Civil List—£15,000 a year on marrying.

The Queen knew, as Drew Middleton wrote, that a marriage under such conditions would be a severe blow to the "delicate relation of Crown, Church and Government." But equally as important was the position in the Commonwealth, held together in the mid-twentieth century by the mystique of the Crown. The Queen is, under the Statute of Westminster passed in 1931, the Queen of each of the Commonwealth countries and, therefore, Princess Margaret, in line to the throne, is a Princess of all the Commonwealth countries, too. If the Princess wished to contract out of her obligations she could do so only as provided for under the statute. Chapter Four states: "Whereas it is meet and proper to set out in the preamble to this Act that inasmuch as the Crown is the symbol of the free association of the Commonwealth of Nations, and as they are united by a common allegiance to the Crown, *it would be in accord with the established constitutional position of all the members of the Commonwealth in relation to one another that any alteration in the law touching the succession to the Throne or the Royal Style and Titles shall hereafter require the assent as well of the Parlia-*

*ments of all the Dominions as of the Parliament of the United Kingdom."*

The Queen did not need her Prime Minister to point out that the marriage which the Princess proposed making would weaken the position of the Crown in the Commonwealth countries. That had been clear during the informal discussions when the Commonwealth Premiers met in London at the time of the Coronation.

Eden bowed himself from the Queen's presence. The elder sister was left with a massive problem. But the hour was perhaps not too late. The Queen was faced with the most unhappy task that she is ever likely to be called upon to undertake. From the moment when Margaret was born on that wild night at Glamis Castle and Elizabeth gave the new-born baby her favorite doll, the elder sister had always tried to insure her little sister's happiness.

Now the Queen had to choose between her duty and her love for her sister. There was no doubt which course the Queen would follow. She knew where her duty lay and she would not shrink from advising Margaret where her duty lay, too. The moment to give that advice was yet to come.

As the Princess was driving home from her cocktail party, Eden was returning to Downing Street from the Palace. Townsend, already back at Lowndes Square, had asked the policeman on duty to tell the reporters that he would not be going out again that night.

The next day, Wednesday, the Princess and Townsend did not meet—it was the first day they had not done so since they had both returned to London.

Immediately after breakfast Townsend left his flat. By chance none of the reporters followed him, so he slipped out of London and went to see his son, Giles, at Eton College.

Meanwhile, the Princess left London by helicopter to present new colors to the 1st Battalion of the Highland Light Infantry at Bulford Camp in Wiltshire. When driving back to the R.A.F. station at Boscombe Down the Rolls Royce collided with a traffic island at the entrance to the station. The off side front wing was crushed and the side and rear of the car were badly damaged. The Princess was slightly shaken.

When the Princess presented the new colors to the Highland Light Infantry she used words that were to prove prophetic. She said:

> "History is not made by a few outstanding actions. It is made remorselessly . . . by devotion to duty, by steadiness in times of anxiety, by discipline in waiting. . . ."

That night the Princess accompanied the Queen, the Duke of Edinburgh, and the Queen Mother to Lambeth Palace for the rededication of the bomb-damaged palace chapel, which had been restored. Afterward the royal party dined with the Archbishop of Canterbury and more than fifty bishops in the palace guardroom.

It was a coincidence, of course, that in the throes of her great dilemma as to whether she should contract a marriage that would meet with the disapproval of the Established Church, the Princess should find herself on this night sitting with the highest dignitaries of that Church. What were her emotions we shall never know. Nor shall we know the feelings of the bishops. It was stressed that the Princess, in reaching her final decision, was free from pressure. That may be strictly the truth, but there are all kinds of pressures. And to attend such a ceremony as she did on this night must have had some effect on her feelings.

The following evening the Princess and Townsend were together again. This time it was for dinner with the faithful Wills family. They went to the whitewashed mews house of Major and Mrs. Wills in Kinnerton Street, in fashionable Belgravia. The Princess arrived first. As she stepped from her Rolls Royce in the narrow street the only spectators were a local dressmaker and two garage hands. Townsend arrived a few minutes later, having been driven from Lowndes Square by his host. This dinner followed the pattern of the first with the Bonham Carters. Soon after midnight they had both gone home—separately.

There was no objection to Margaret and Townsend's being seen together in public, although it is a little difficult to understand by what mental processes a decision was reached forbidding them such freedom.

This Thursday was an important day because it had been intimated to the Prime Minister, Sir Anthony Eden, that there seemed little possibility that the Princess would change her mind. At ten-thirty the Cabinet began to meet in Downing Street.

Half an hour after the Ministers had assembled in the green and cream Cabinet room of No. 10 overlooking the Horse Guards Parade, the Attorney-General, Sir Manningham Buller, who was conducting a case in the Queen's Bench Division, was given a message summoning him to Downing Street. He broke off his speech and told the Lord Chief Justice, Lord Goddard: "I have been sent for and am required immediately." Lord Goddard gave him permission to leave the Court.

Sir Reginald drove straight to Downing Street and was immediately ushered into the Cabinet room.

The Attorney-General remained at Downing Street for more than an hour. The Prime Minister intimated to his Ministers that he understood that it was still the desire of Princess Margaret to marry Group Captain Townsend. Consideration was, therefore, immediately given to the terms of a Bill of Renunciation, that would be placed before Parliament to relieve the Princess of her responsibilities under the Royal Marriages Act.

That afternoon, the Socialist opposition "Shadow" Cabinet met under the chairmanship of Mr. Hugh Gaitskell. He informed his colleagues that he understood that the Princess had decided to marry Townsend and that a statement would be made to Parliament early the next week, probably on Tuesday.

After the meeting of the Cabinet, Admiral of the Fleet Earl Mountbatten, the First Sea Lord, with Lady Mountbatten went to lunch at 10 Downing Street with Sir Anthony and Lady Eden.

The political tension was building up. But the Princess remained resolute.

On Thursday afternoon she opened a new outpatient department at Epsom District Hospital. In the children's ward she saw Gillian Cox who was only nineteen months old. Gillian put out her tongue which had healed after being cut by a fall. Margaret joked: "That's one place you can't put a bandage on."

The routine on Friday was much the same. Townsend remained most of the day in the Lowndes Square flat. His tailor, Mr. Stuart Clegg, called during the morning to fit a suit.

In the morning the Princess attended the unveiling by the Queen of the National Memorial to her father, King George VI, in Carlton Gardens, overlooking the Mall. Photographs of her walking behind the Queen Mother showed her smiling and looking happy.

In the afternoon she had an engagement at the East India Docks. And that night she was again with Townsend. This time they dined by candlelight at the home of Mr. and Mrs. Michael Brand, at a three-storied Georgian house in St. Leonard's Terrace, Chelsea. Mr. Brand, a dealer in rare books, and his wife, a sister of Viscount Hambleden, were old friends of the Princess who was a godmother to their son.

Mrs. Brand was formerly the Honorable Laura Smith and her wedding in July, 1953, was attended by the Queen Mother, Princess Margaret, and the Duchess of Kent. To Mrs. Brand the Princess gave one of her personal seats in Westminster Abbey for the Coronation. Before her marriage she was often in the Princess' theater parties.

On this evening the Princess wore a dress of royal blue with gold piping. Again she arrived before Townsend. This time he was driven by Michael Brand.

It was one o'clock before the Princess left St. Leonard's Terrace. As she came out in the early morning rain she wrapped a mink stole around her shoulders. A few sightseers had waited for many hours to see her.

Her sister, the Queen, had dined that evening with the Admirals of the Royal Navy in the Painted Hall of the Royal Naval College at Greenwich.

On Saturday evening Townsend again spent an hour or so with the Princess at Clarence House. This must have been a vital meeting. The next day the Princess was to spend with the Queen and Prince Philip at Windsor Castle. And yet it would appear from subsequent events that when Townsend went back to Lowndes Square he knew that the Princess was unwavering in her determination.

It was now more than a week since Townsend had arrived back in London. The newspapers had dogged the footsteps of both the Princess and himself, struggling to make significant gossip of every transient expression. But the titillating will-she-or-won't-she speculation of the keyhole-peepers had become only a tinkling obligato behind sterner voices.

Whatever else the British royal family may be in modern Britain—symbol of legitimacy, shining emblem of Commonwealth unity, indestructible warranty of the glory that is Britain—it is first and foremost a family affair: every spinster is its maiden aunt, every shopgirl its happily envious kid sister, every vicar its parish priest, and every family man its authoritative uncle. In moments of relative calm, the country cousins can watch and enjoy the cavorting of their royal relations in London with the detachment of television viewers watching a soap opera. But when the affairs in Britain's *One Man's Family* take critical turns—as they had during this week in London—the detachment vanishes.

In the press and pulpit, in the pub and the barbershop, in

the family parlor and the public park, the British people were voicing their sympathy, their shock, their approval, their disapproval, or their angry impatience at the whole affair.

The circumstances were becoming familiar enough to permit a few small and very English jokes about it. In *Punch,* then under editorship of Malcolm Muggeridge, critic of royalty, was a cartoon depicting an impressionable child thoughtfully counting the peas on her plate to the words, "Tinker, tailor, soldier, group captain." A B.B.C. comedian asked his straight man to read the day's news. "They had tea together again," intoned the other.

But back of the little jokes and the large admonitions, a disquieting uncertainty hung over the nation—an uncertainty not dissimilar to that of the fateful days in December, 1936, the hours before Edward gave up his throne.

It would be untrue to suggest that anybody in Britain expected that the Princess' romance with her divorced commoner would end in the collapse of the British throne, or believed it would cause more than a passing disruption in Anthony Eden's government. Not even the defection of Salisbury could have done that. What it could do, and some felt had already done, was to damage a faith already weakened by repeated blows.

Britons in the postwar years lacked something of their old self-confidence. The advent of a young Queen, the brave talk of a new Elizabethan era, the dynamic character of a new self-confident Toryism (to be found ephemeral), the conquest of Everest by Edmund Hillary, and of time by four-minute miler Roger Bannister, were all factors combining to bolster that waning confidence.

In this no longer gay romance, there were no villains, only victims. What modern Britons had come to demand and need most of all from their royal family was example. As the *Times* was to put it: "The Queen has come to be the symbol . . . in whom the people see their better selves ideally reflected." But there was a corollary: in reflecting the national idea, the monarchy must not set itself apart and away from the people it represents. The reflection must be that of normality clothed in ermine, and while the institution remains beyond reproach, the wearers of the ermine must show themselves warm and human beneath. But when romance conflicts with the canons of the Established Church, and with the nation's inbred view of royalty, it is no easy role.

In times past, ringed about as they were with lords and ladies dependent on their favor, without the popular press to discuss their romances as they would Rita Hayworth's, the sovereigns of England could afford to be human without fear of the consequences. Worry over his subjects' approval was fairly far from the mind of King Henry VIII when he divorced his wife, Catherine of Aragon, in favor of Anne Boleyn. As we have seen earlier, the mistresses and mismarriages of the first royal Hanovers newly come from Germany were far more scandalous than the prospect that scandalized some churchgoing Britons in the autumn of 1955. In previous days royalty operated behind a bulwark of aristocracy that fenced it off safely from the people.

The modern respect for the monarch began with the long reign of Queen Victoria. Her five daughters were brought up in a court peopled with carefully sifted members of a nobility as rigidly aloof as the sovereign herself.

The monarchy into which Princess Margaret was born was still securely bound in the tradition of Queen Victoria. Six years later it was dealt a severe blow by the abdication of King Edward VIII, now Duke of Windsor. Those who sought in the Margaret-Townsend crisis to draw a parallel with that Crown crisis were wrong. There was not much to compare in the two. Edward was the King-Emperor, the personal embodiment of the sovereign power in a Britain still governed by Victorian standards. Margaret was a Princess in a predominantly socialist-minded State, and with little hope of ascending the throne.

As we have seen, when Edward chose the course of abdication, six-year-old Margaret herself asked with wide eyes: "Are they going to chop off his head?" It was not necessary. In choosing to give up his throne, Edward made himself, in the eyes of some Englishmen, something less than a man without a head. The people let him go, and anointed his conscientious younger brother George, Margaret's father.

This leads one to just this thought: When England was subjected to the first real threat of cross-Channel conquest since 1066, King George looked for his protection not to the armored earls and barons of his ancestors but to a new aristocracy of young men flying Spitfires and Hurricanes. And one of their brightest stars was twenty-five-year-old Peter Townsend.

After Townsend had left Clarence House on Saturday evening, Princess Margaret drove to Windsor Castle. The next day, with her sister and Prince Philip, she attended divine service at the Chapel Royal. After lunch the Queen and her husband sat and talked with Margaret before a log fire in the green drawing room of the Victoria Tower, Windsor Castle.

This was the first occasion during the crisis—and it was to be the last—for the three to discuss alone the family problem.

There is no evidence, and I do not think there was any at that important meeting, that either the Queen or Prince Philip exerted extreme pressure on Princess Margaret. But the Queen, in doing her duty as she saw it, would have to review the full consequences to the Princess and the possible consequences to the Crown of the proposed marriage.

What could have taken place at that meeting on Sunday afternoon at Windsor Castle? It is safe to conjecture that it was agreed that if the Princess married Townsend it should be a civil marriage. I have always understood that the Princess assured her sister that this type of ceremony was also the wish of Townsend.

It was further agreed that Parliament should be asked to pass a Bill which would strip the Princess of all her royal obligations and that she would forfeit her income under the Civil List.

The latter created complications. How were the couple to live after marriage? Contrary to general belief, the Princess is not a rich woman in her own right. She has inherited money from both her grandmother, Queen Mary, and her father. But the income from this capital would not have been sufficient for the newly married couple to live on the lavish scale to which Margaret had been accustomed.

The Queen had to point out to her sister that Townsend was an officer serving in the Royal Air Force, dependent largely on his service pay and allowances. He had no other job and had been trained for none. If he married the Princess it might be embarrassing for both of them if he stayed on in the Air Force. But what would he do if he retired from the Service? These were unpleasant truths but they had to be faced.

Further, it seemed difficult to see how the couple could live in England—at least for some while—after their marriage. Many complications would arise. Townsend as a divorced man could not go into the Royal Enclosure at Ascot. Nor could he attend state banquets at the Palace if the Queen wished to invite her sister.

And yet, in spite of all these obstacles, the Princess had to tell her sister and brother-in-law that she was too deeply in love with Townsend to give him up. Therefore, the die seemed cast.

Thus began a new week of suspense for the people. Surely the decision could not now be long delayed?

On Monday afternoon Townsend spent ninety minutes with the Princess alone at Clarence House. Presumably she told him what had passed between her and her sister and brother-in-law. It is my belief that Townsend now began to have doubts about the wisdom of their contemplated marriage. Could they be happy if they married under the conditions which were being imposed? Had he the right to ask the Princess, born of royal estate, to give it all up and become an ordinary woman? Would their love be strong enough to endure the years of strain that would be imposed upon them by the restrictions under which their marriage would take place? Would not the Princess in time feel that their marriage offended her religious conscience? Also there was the problem of Communion, to which the Princess must attach much importance.

There was one more argument. That morning, the fact that the Princess could not have her royal cake and eat it too, had been brought home to her with the force of a thunderbolt. When she opened her *Times*—which up to then had maintained a stern silence on her romance—she read that wedlock with a divorced man would mean her "entering into a union which vast numbers of her sister's people, all sincerely anxious for her life-long happiness, *cannot in all conscience regard as a marriage.*"

The timing of the publication of this article was quite brilliant. The Editor of the *Times* knew from sources in the Palace and the Government that the hour of decision was fast approaching. All means had been used to dissuade the Princess. They had proved of no avail. Love, apparently, was too strong. But the *Times,* with its vast experience of influencing decisions, knew that this was the moment when the voice of authority—the Crown, the Church, and the Government—should be heard by the people.

Any narrative of the Margaret-Townsend Story, must, therefore, quote in full this historic editorial. It is a piece of contemporary history. This is what the *Times* said:

> "In the mounting tumult over the assumed wish of the Queen's sister to marry a gallant officer, with nothing to his disadvantage except that his divorced wife is still living, few if any persons holding responsible positions in the Commonwealth have yet expressed an opinion. Their reasons for reti-

cence are clear: they know little, and they care too much. But now that the reckless magnification of mere guesses has gone so far that the name of the Princess is being bandied about, sometimes in heartless and offensive contexts, far beyond the confines of the British Commonwealth, it will soon be necessary for all who care for the monarchy to form some tentative judgment, even if it must for the time being rest partly upon hypothesis.

"The enormous popular emotion that has been generated by the recent happenings is in itself perfectly healthy. It is sentimental; it is ill-informed; but it proceeds from that genuine affection for the Royal Family which they have inherited and continue to deserve, and which is a principal guarantee of the stability of Kingdom and Commonwealth. The odious whipping-up of these honest and warmhearted feelings, and their vulgar exploitation for motives of gain, have already dishonoured part of the British Press in the eyes of the world, and deserve only contempt. Though this mass sentiment would be a gratifying proof of the soundness of our institutions if it were allowed to be spontaneous, the only help it can give the Princess in a matter of conscience is the assurance that her choice matters greatly to untold millions of people. For a personal concern can seldom be a private concern when the person is royal; it is part of the sacrifice the whole Royal Family make to the ideal they represent, that they must live their private lives largely in public. Yet personal the choice remains; what is at issue is the future direction of a life, hitherto dedicated. That can be determined only by Princess Margaret herself; the inner responsibility can in no way be lightened by any weight of mass opinion, however sympathetic, on one side or the other.

"Neither can Her Royal Highness's ultimate decision be much helped, or seriously hindered, by posing the issue in harshly legalistic light. At present, it is true, the suggested marriage is forbidden by the law of the State without the permission of the Queen, who is its head, and by the accredited authorities of the Church of England, of which she is Supreme Governor. But there is a procedure by which the Princess might release herself from the rigour of the Royal

Marriages Act, and the Act itself would be easily set aside by
Parliament if it were generally felt that the crucial matter
was merely the capacity of the Princess and her issue, in a
remote eventuality, to inherit the Crown. The teaching of
the Church of England on divorce comes much nearer the
heart of the matter, but again not quite for the technical reasons that have in some places been advanced. If the objection
to the marriage on these grounds derived solely from the constitutional fact that the Queen is Governor of the Church, it
would be relevant only to that southern part of the United
Kingdom in which the Church of England is established. But
the dilemma is felt, and rightly felt, to be the concern of all
the Queen's subjects throughout the Commonwealth, each
kingdom of which regards not only Her Majesty herself but
the Royal Family as an integral part of its own community.
The truth is that the public factor in the Princess's personal
problem is introduced by something which is neither Church
nor State, but a living organism which is broader and more
profoundly based than either, but less easily definable in lawyer's terms. That organism is the many-sided society or family of the Queen's subjects, of which Church and State are no
more than ecclesiastical and political aspects.

"Now, in the Twentieth-Century conception of the monarchy, the Queen has come to be the symbol of every side of
life of this society, its universal representative in whom her
people see their better selves ideally reflected; and since part
of their ideal is of family life, the Queen's family has its own
part in the reflection. If the marriage which is now being
discussed comes to pass, it is inevitable that this reflection becomes distorted. *The Princess will be entering* into a union
which vast numbers of her sister's people, all sincerely *anxious for her life-long happiness, cannot in conscience regard
as a marriage.* This opinion would be held whether the
Church of England were established or not, and extends to
great bodies of Christians outside it. That devout men have
argued that it is a wrong interpretation of Christianity is
not here relevant. All that matters is that it is widely and
sincerely held; and therefore that a royal marriage which
flouted it would cause acute division among loyal subjects

everywhere. But the Royal Family is above all things the symbol and guarantee of the unity of the British peoples; if one of its members herself becomes a cause of division, the salt has lost its savour.

"There is no escape from the logic of the situation. The Queen's sister married to a divorced man (even though the innocent party) *would be irrevocably disqualified from playing her part in the essential royal function*—a part, be it said, which she has hitherto played with the utmost charm and devotion. On the other hand, the royal service to the people would lose most of its grace if it were felt to be conscript service; nor can representation of a people's unity be sustained with a divided heart. If the Princess finally decides, with all the anxious deliberation that clearly she has given to her problem, that she is unable to make the sacrifice involved in her continued dedication to her inherited part, then she has a right to lay down a burden that is too heavy for her. It would, however, involve withdrawal, not merely from her formal rights in the succession established by law, together with such official duties as sometimes fall to her under the Regency Acts, but *abandonment of her place in the Royal Family as a group fulfilling innumerable symbolic and representative functions.* If she decided to ask Parliament to release her from so much of these as is legal obligation, she would from that moment pass into private life, and it would become an impertinence for anybody to criticise the way she then chooses to order her personal affairs.

"But the peoples of the Commonwealth would see her step down from her high place with the deepest regret, for she has adorned it, and is everywhere honoured and loved. Moreover, there would be profound sympathy with the Queen, who would be left still more lonely in her arduous life of public service in which she needs all the support and cooperation that only her close kindred can give. These things said, the matter is, in the last resort, one to be determined solely by Princess Margaret's conscience. Whatever the judgment of that unsparing tribunal, her fellow-subjects will wish her every possible happiness—not forgetting that happiness in the full sense is a spiritual state, and *that its most precious element may be the sense of duty done.*"

On Monday evening, for the fourth time, the Princess and Townsend dined with friends. This time it was at the home of Mr. and Mrs. John Lowther, in Victoria Road, Kensington. Mrs. Lowther was formerly Miss Jennifer Bevan, Princess Margaret's first Lady-in-Waiting. The other guests were Mr. and Mrs. Michael Brand who had entertained the couple on Friday night.

The party broke up at twelve-thirty.

The next afternoon Townsend again went to Clarence House. Fifteen minutes before he arrived the Queen Mother went off to the Dairy Show. She arrived back home half an hour before Townsend left.

Again Margaret and Townsend spent the afternoon discussing their situation. And again there was no final decision. But the Princess was undoubtedly beginning to waver.

Earlier in the day she had looked very happy when she went to meet the President of Portugal, General Lopes, at Westminster Bridge. She wore a velvet coat of vivid royal blue and a toque hat of pale blue feathers. She had five strands of pearls.

Soon after Townsend left Clarence House, the President of Portugal called on the Queen Mother.

That night, the Princess, a resplendent figure, attended the state banquet at Buckingham Palace for General Lopes.

Wednesday, October 26, was the day of decision.

There were other voices in the land equally as stern as that of the *Times*. The contemplated marriage, said an Episcopal minister in Scotland, would be "an illicit union . . . adding something very like the sin of apostasy to the violation of Christ's marriage law." Dr. Leslie Weatherhead, President of the Methodist Conference, was the first important Church leader to comment directly on the future of the Princess. In a statement he said:

"Princess Margaret and Group Captain Townsend are popular young people in love with one another, and everyone would wish that they could have the right of any other young British couple and find happiness.

"But clearly the status of the British Princess raises difficulties in regard to a fiancé who is divorced and whose wife and two children are living.

"Should anything—an aeroplane accident, for instance, unfortunately end the lives of Prince Charles and Princess Anne, or if they both died without issue, then at Princess Margaret's death her eldest child would be heir to the Throne.

"Yet that child would be the fruit of a marriage which many Anglicans would not recognise as valid.

"This is bound to be a matter of vital public concern, for, among other things, such an heir would be doomed to disapproval or worse in the eyes of many people of this realm.

"*If the State Church approved this marriage, it would break its own rules.*

"If, however, Princess Margaret renounced all claims to the Throne for herself and her issue, then she would be free, in the eyes of many, to enjoy married happiness with Group Captain Townsend, though even then, her example does not make it easier to uphold the ideal of Christian marriage in a land in which divorce is already too lightly regarded, homes too readily broken up, and children too thoughtlessly deprived of the mental security of having two united parents, a security which surely is part of God's plan."

And the Archbishop of Canterbury, on the same day, also intervened. At a meeting of the British Council of Churches, over which he was presiding in Manchester, he was asked if there had been any move in the Church of England to change its attitude toward the remarriage of divorced persons.

Dr. Fisher replied: "A reasonable church does not change its teaching every few minutes."

To this Mr. A. P. Herbert, the father of the Divorce Bill of 1937, promptly retorted: ". . . The Church of England has changed; and, under other leaders, may change again one day."

Mr. Herbert then quoted the great Mendell Creighton, Bishop of London from 1897 to 1901: "We as Christians abhor divorce; but when a divorce has been judged necessary are we to refuse any liberty to the innocent or wronged party. I could not advise any of my clergy to refuse to solemnise a marriage of an innocent party who genuinely desired God's blessing. *I prefer to err on the side of charity.*"

And then Mr. Herbert quoted the late Archbishop Temple, who stated: "The Book of Common Prayer, where alone the authentic teaching of the Church may be found, does not pronounce marriage indissoluble." Mr. Herbert also quoted Archbishop Randall Davidson, who denied that subsequent marriage after divorce was sinful or that the solemnization in church of such a marriage was a condonation of sin.

But not all the voices of propriety on that morning in October, 1955, spoke in such severe terms. The liberal *Manchester Guardian,* which speaks with equal authority, replied to the *Times* with an earnest question. "Is the democratic instinct of the country in this Twentieth Century," it asked, "really in favour of hedging royalty in with ecclesiastical prescriptions of arguable historical and theological validity? Or does it not rather prefer to give royalty the same rights and freedom in their personal affairs as ordinary, decent citizens?"

To the troubled Princess and Peter Townsend, it was small comfort that there were some who tried to dismiss the whole matter as a moss-backed anachronism. The ever-cocky *Daily Mirror* (circulation four million plus) rushed to the defense by asking its more influential brother (circulation two hundred thousand plus): "Would *The Times* have preferred this vivacious young woman to marry one of the witless wonders with whom she has been hobnobbing these past few years? Or to live her life in devoted spinsterhood? Luckily *The Times* cannot banish Princess Margaret. It speaks for a dusty world and a forgotten age."

Nobody knew better than the Princess, who was trained to her station, that monarchy's duty to please the majority often consists in not offending the influential minority, especially when the minority stands on time-honored tradition. She could only hope that if she married outside the Established Church in a civil ceremony, even the Church itself might in time prove forgiving. Had not the Archbishop of Canterbury written: "I do not find myself able to forbid good people who come to me for advice to embark on a second marriage. I tell them that it is their duty as conscientiously as they can to decide before God what they should do."

There was no chance that Parliament would make the Princess' lot easier by so amending the Royal Marriages Act as to eliminate the necessity of a choice. The alternatives before the Princess—and, of course, Townsend—had become hard and clear. The hour had come for a painful choice.

Just before six o'clock on Wednesday evening—twenty minutes after the Princess arrived home from a visit to Seaford, followed by the Queen Mother—Townsend called again at Clarence House. When he went to this meeting he must have been convinced that their marriage was not a workable proposition. The Princess was, surely, equally convinced.

This must have been the most distressing ninety minutes that this young couple would ever be called upon to have together. No longer could the decision be postponed. To do so could only embarrass the Princess' family.

The couple at last recognized that it was not in the best interests of the Crown and of the Princess for the marriage to take place. They were deeply in love with each other, but could their marriage in such controversial circumstances bring the lasting happiness to them (and to their children) which in the full sense is a spiritual state? The obstacles seemed insurmountable. The ultimate decision had to be the Princess' but it required the courage of a man to help her reach that final conclusion. There is no doubt—in fact, the

Princess made it clear in her communiqué—that Peter gave her the necessary courage. And that does not detract from the sacrifice which this young woman made by putting duty before love.

At the end of ninety minutes the marriage was off. If this distressed couple were near to tears it would not be surprising.

After a few minutes, the Queen Mother was asked to join them. They told her of their brave decision. And that night the Princess' sister, the Queen, knew when all the royal family went to a state dinner at the Portuguese Embassy that Princess Margaret had chosen the path of duty.

But, even if the Princess and Townsend had taken the decision which so many had prayed for, there was in their decision a condition which filled the family with apprehension. The Princess insisted on issuing a communiqué which would make it clear to all the world that she loved Group Captain Townsend and that she would *always* love him. Further, she insisted that she and Townsend should spend one more weekend in a friend's house before they parted.

The latter proposal was agreed to and it was further agreed that the ideal family for them to stay with should be Lord Rupert Nevill and his wife—friends of both the royal family and Townsend—at Uckfield in Sussex.

But the battle over the statement by the Princess was not over and was to continue for many days.

The following afternoon, Thursday, Princess Margaret drove to Lambeth Palace to see the Archbishop of Canterbury. Dr. Fisher, to keep the appointment, canceled, at short notice, a long-arranged engagement to present prizes at a Canterbury school. Officially he announced he had changed his arrangements in order to deal with "State affairs." It was inevitable that the press should state that there was little doubt that the Princess had gone to Lambeth Palace to consult the Archbishop, spiritual head of the Established Church, about the attitude of the Church, of which the Queen is temporal Governor, about marriage problems—in particular the ecclesiastical veto on the marriage of divorced persons in the Church of England.

But the press was wrong. The Princess had made up her mind not to marry Group Captain Townsend before she went to see the Archbishop.

Dr. Fisher, no doubt supposing that the Princess was coming to consult him, had all his books of reference spread around him, carefully marked and cross-referenced.

When the Princess entered his library, she said, in words worthy of Queen Elizabeth I: "My Lord Archbishop, you may put away your books. I have made up my mind already."

The Princess then told Dr. Fisher of her decision.

That night, Princess Margaret, in a tiara and strapless pink and white gown, helped her sister the Queen to entertain the visiting President of Portugal in a box at Covent Garden, by sitting through a performance of Smetana's *The Bartered Bride,* while a soprano sang to a forbidden lover, "Nothing in the world will ever part us."

When the orchestra played "God Save the Queen" and the Portuguese national anthem, the Princess was photographed in the royal box standing apart from the other occupants. It was a remarkable picture. Her face bore the impassive dignity that is royalty's required uniform.

Some persons the next morning interpreted her regal look as one of defiance of convention. They were certain that she would go through with her proposed marriage. But, of course, in the knowledge of hindsight, it was a woman telling the world that she had chosen the path of duty instead of love.

And while the Princess was at the opera, Peter Townsend was alone with his thoughts in the flat at Lowndes Square.

On Friday morning the Queen presided over a meeting of the Privy Council at Buckingham Palace. Then the Duke of Edinburgh drove to Northolt airport to fly himself in a four-engined Heron of the Queen's to Scotland. And it also became known that the Queen was to travel by the overnight train to join her husband.

But before the Queen left, a sad-faced Princess, during the afternoon, went to Buckingham Palace to see her sister.

About the same time the Queen Mother drove from Clarence House to the Royal Lodge in Windsor Great Park.

What could all this mean? Surely this exodus of the royal family from London must mean that the Princess had decided to marry Townsend. Reporters were tapping every source for news. Some with contacts in Court circles were puzzled when it was hinted that the Princess had done the equivalent of "leaving home." It was even said that a van containing twenty pieces of luggage had already gone ahead of her to Uckfield House. And yet, of course, all this gossip was completely untrue.

During the afternoon Townsend drove to Eridge Castle, the home of the Marquess of Abergavenny near Tunbridge Wells. It had been arranged that he should sleep at the Castle over the weekend and visit the Princess during the day at Uckfield House. He drove to Uckfield for dinner on Friday evening and after the meal he and the Princess were left alone to consider the terms of the statement which she wished to issue.

Until the early hours of the morning the two talked about the wording of the communiqué. Sentences were scribbled on pieces of paper, only to be torn up. But at last they agreed on what they would say. Most of the words were written by Townsend, who, in moments of deep emotion, has a flare for the right phrase.

By the time that the draft was complete, it was too late for Townsend to go back to Eridge Castle. It was arranged that he should not leave Uckfield House over the weekend. And this was a more sensible arrangement, it was felt, because the whole of the estate was cordoned inside by police and outside by reporters.

On Saturday afternoon, after the Princess and Townsend had walked hand in hand in the garden during the morning, Captain Oliver Dawnay, the Queen Mother's Private Secretary, arrived at Uckfield to receive the draft communiqué. But this thirty-five-year-old ex-Guards officer came as more than a messenger. He was instructed by the Queen and the Queen Mother—on the advice of Commander Colville, the Queen's Press Secretary—to make a last-minute attempt to persuade the Princess *not* to issue a statement. On this the Princess was adamant.

Dawnay drove back to London.

Sunday came. Hundreds of cars with sightseers descended on the small Sussex town in the hope of seeing the Princess go to church. In the lane that leads up to the main gate of Uckfield House, the crowds even brought out lunchtime picnic baskets. Others lit camp stoves to heat up soup. At the fourteenth-century church at Frant, eleven miles away, where they expected the Princess for morning service, the brasses were polished, fresh chrysanthemum blooms decorated the altar, and the church was filled. But the Princess did not leave Uckfield House. Nor did Townsend.

For a while during the morning, on the terrace that surrounds the red brick Queen Anne style mansion, children of Lord and Lady Rupert Nevill played with an orange ball. Shortly afterward the Princess and Townsend again strolled in the garden.

Dawnay arrived back on Sunday afternoon. This time he was instructed by the Queen and the Queen Mother to secure the deletion of one word. Margaret had insisted on the inclusion of a sentence—written by herself—which read: "I have been strengthened by the unfailing support and devotion of Group Captain Townsend." Dawnay tactfully explained that it would be better if the word "devotion" were omitted. Margaret dug her toes in. It is even said that she threatened to go back on her decision and marry Townsend unless the communiqué was issued exactly as she and the Group Captain had drafted it.

The Palace bowed to her wishes.

Sunday evening was the last evening that the Princess and Peter Townsend were to spend alone. Again she played the piano to him and again they talked. Afterward, friends of the royal family said that the Princess made a promise to Townsend which explains so much of what has happened since. The Princess said she was too deeply in love with him ever to marry anyone else. And that was why she was insistent that her statement to be issued on the morrow should make this abundantly clear.

There is no reason to believe that Townsend accepted such a promise. It would not have been fair of him to ask her to remain unmarried. And, as proof of this, he left England for two years. By doing so, he gave her complete freedom; he could not then be accused of interfering in her life in any way.

The Princess agreed that in order to satisfy public opinion it was better that he go away. But it would not alter her feelings toward him, nor would it alter her intention not to marry anyone else.

Peter Townsend probably knew that this was not the time to argue with the Princess. He must have hoped that with the passage of time she would find lasting happiness with another man.

On Monday morning the Princess drove back to London and shortly afterward Townsend went too.

And during the day the Queen and Prince Philip returned to London from Scotland and the Queen Mother from Windsor.

The hour was now growing late. To the outside world the situation was nearing, it seemed, the point of crisis. The world was busily chattering and gossiping about the Princess' affairs. As the afternoon wore on there was an air of certainty that the decision would be known in a few hours. Few, however, doubted the outcome: The Princess would marry her airman.

At teatime—that all-important hour to all Britons—the Group Captain set out from Lowndes Square in his green Renault for his last drive to Clarence House.

Soon afterward the Princess issued her statement of simple dignity and sincerity, and also of remarkable candor. It dispelled any possible doubts—as she was determined it should—that she deeply loved Group Captain Townsend. But after three weeks of torment she had taken the *irrevocable* step. She had surrendered the love of her life because of her religious faith and her duty to the Commonwealth.

This was her statement:

> "I would like it to be known that I have decided not to marry Group Captain Townsend. I have been aware that, subject to my renouncing my rights of succession, it might have been possible for me to contract a civil marriage. But, mindful of the Church's teachings that Christian marriage is indissoluble, and conscious of my duty to the Commonwealth, I have resolved to put these considerations before others. I have reached this decision entirely alone, and in doing so I have been strengthened by the unfailing support and devotion of Group Captain Townsend. I am deeply grateful for the concern of all those who have constantly prayed for my happiness.
>
> "(Signed)   Margaret.
>
> "Monday, October 31, 1955."

Princess Margaret had rescued the royal family from a difficult situation. Perhaps she could not hope to silence the gossipmongers and the tittle-tattlers. But nevertheless, she and Townsend have had to endure the talk as the years have gone by, although it cannot be denied that they both protected the dignity and prestige of the throne.

Peter Townsend had been the subject of much misrepresentation. He still is. But if that Monday evening meant his going back into the shadows, he went with his own self-respect intact. Throughout those painful nineteen days he had borne himself with remarkable restraint and dignity.

At six seventeen, pale and tense, Townsend drove from Clarence House to Lowndes Square. A few minutes later he came out and asked a reporter to guide him out of London toward Sussex. This time there was no police escort.

Within seconds of the issuance of the communiqué it was flashed round the world. The B.B.C. broke into their radio and television services to give the news. In the Commonwealth countries and in America and throughout Europe the decision was broadcast immediately.

The Princess remained that evening with her mother at Clarence House while her sister and Prince Philip went to the Royal Film Show.

The immediate reaction of Britons to Princess Margaret's dignified statement was a buzz everywhere of "I told you so," "What a shame," or "She did the right thing."

As the days wore on, the discussion was to show some signs of developing in many quarters into soul-searching national self-examination. But that was later, after the first signs of disappointment from those who had favored the marriage— and there were many—and the "ouffs" of relief from those who had opposed it.

The "ouff" of the *Times* was as lordly as its blast against the marriage the week before. In neither of the two editorials did the newspaper mention the name of Group Captain Peter Townsend. The nearest the writer came to it was "gallant officer."

"All the peoples of the Commonwealth," wrote the *Times* on Tuesday morning, "will feel gratitude to her for taking the selfless, royal way which in their hearts they expected of her." The weekly *Time and Tide* struck the same note: "Love itself means less today because duty has come to mean so little . . . it has come as a salutory shock to many that she made the sterner decision in favour of duty." Commented the *Church Times:* "She has done the plain duty laid on every loyal member of the Church." The Conservative *Daily Telegraph,* which had always taken the line that the whole thing was almost as absurd as it was improper, judged curtly, "outsiders may well feel that conscience has been the ally of commonsense." From the Tory *Daily Mail* came: "Who can doubt that the Princess has made the right decision?" The Church of England newspaper came out with a full-page portrait of a smiling Margaret, under the headline: "Princess Margaret: Life begins anew."

And yet conservative opinion, although it judged that a marriage would have been a great evil, was aware that the long period of official silence and mishandling, the glare which had revealed confusion in high places and inconsistencies between the law of the realm and the rulings of its official Church, could perhaps spell danger to established authority. A great movement to close the ranks became apparent.

Said the *Daily Mail:* "One institution emerges calm, serene and unshaken . . . the British Monarchy . . . today stands stronger than ever, rooted in the hearts of a great people. It is strong enough to confront with superb, silent indifference the frantic bawlings of superficial opinion."

However, the British monarchy could not survive without the support of superficial opinion, some of which showed uneasiness and even anger over the dramatic denouement. The *Daily Mirror* and the *Daily Express*—with their estimated combined daily readership of twenty-five millions—amply demonstrated this.

Lord Beaverbrook's *Express* prophesied "dismay and perplexity at Princess Margaret's moving message to the nation . . . the decision has been reached amid a pressure campaign that would have brought to their knees even more determined personalities than she. . . . How could any girl fail to be influenced by so much opposition? . . . Her statement shows unmistakably that they [her feelings for Townsend] have not changed. And that she would marry him tomorrow if she felt able to. . . . The pity is that she would give up so much when neither right nor morality demands it."

The *Daily Mirror* boldly announced that it did not care to join "in the suffocating chant of 'Good show!' "; and worried lest the powers who got their own way would now continue their persecution of Peter Townsend. "It is customary in these islands for people who have become socially embarrassing to be spirited out of the country . . . the Commonwealth is well-stocked with minor jobs in far-flung countries for people whose presence here would be inconvenient. Without doubt the magnifying glasses are out in Whitehall today as bureaucrats search for unlikely places at the end of the earth where Peter Townsend can be banished. This must not happen."

London's other tabloid, the *Daily Sketch,* torn between its political affiliations (it belongs to Lord Rothermere) and the knowledge that most people were upset by the unhappy ending to the romance, clung to its Conservative loyalties while managing to surpass anything in the way of embarrassing journalism yet attempted: "A tear falls on a page of history," it declared. "For God and for the Commonwealth. These are the causes for which her love is lost . . . she has given dignity and meaning to the fact of being a woman, and every woman in this country who has the right to call herself English is enriched by her action."

From the *Manchester Guardian* came this reasoned and ominous criticism: ". . . None the less her decision, which has plainly been come to after subtle pressure, will be regarded by great masses of people as unnecessary and perhaps a great waste. In the long run it will not redound to the credit or influence of those who have been most persistent in denying the Princess the same liberty that is enjoyed by the rest of her fellow-citizens. Even the least cynical among us find it hard to see why an innocent party to a divorce can become the man who appoints Archbishops and Bishops [i.e., Sir Anthony Eden], while the Princess, who merely exercises her social graces and has a very remote chance of succeeding to the Throne, should be denied by ecclesiastical prescription the right to marry an innocent party to a divorce. That odd piece of inconsistency may be typically English, but it has more than a smack of English hypocrisy about it."

The ideological Left Wing had no doubt about where it stood: "The Archbishops," warned Francis Williams, Press Officer for Lord Attlee when he was Prime Minister, "may yet live to wonder whether their present victory has not been won at heavy cost." And the Bevanite Michael Foot, in the *Tribune,* was even more outspoken: ". . . One good may come from the whole episode. The Royal racket, sustained alike by both the pompous and the yellow press . . . may lose some of its appeal and commercial value. Let's hope so . . . a republican party may still be reborn in England."

Into Fleet Street there poured thousands of letters, most of them expressing deep and widespread resentment. But behind the thousands who wrote, there were the millions who did not. Most of them admired Princess Margaret's decision, without perhaps being quite sure where lay right or wrong.

But it was not the royal family which was under direct fire, but the Church and the Archbishop of Canterbury. Unfairly he was credited with being the person responsible for having changed the Princess' mind. However, he did make the tactical error of indirectly or clumsily replying to his critics.

He chose as his medium a seemingly casual visit to Lambeth Palace by a B.B.C. television unit conducted by Richard Dimbleby, a most popular and ineffably pompous radio commentator. When Dimbleby casually remarked: "I imagine most people in the country must think you were very closely connected with Princess Margaret's decision," the Archbishop replied that he wanted to "underline" some points, two of which were that Margaret made her decision "purely on grounds of conscience," and that "she took this decision alone, and that means of her own free will." Naïvely the Archbishop spoiled the effect of the latter remark by adding, "of course, she took advice, and she chose who she took her advice from, and she got plenty of advice asked for and a good deal unasked for."

Later, as Dr. Fisher was showing Dimbleby some portraits of past Archbishops, the pair stopped with studied casualness before the picture of Dr. Lang, who was Archbishop of Canterbury at the time of King Edward's abdication. Dr. Fisher remarked that, despite popular gossip to the effect that Dr. Lang had been much concerned with the events surrounding the abdication, "he had no part in it and was not consulted up to the time of the abdication."

Dimbleby's comment: "Archbishops seem made to be maligned." Dr. Fisher chuckled and answered, "As far as I am concerned, I don't care two hoots." He claimed that "We are the only people looking to see what effect this business of divorce will have on the nation in five or ten years. We are fighting against a great popular wave of stupid emotionalism. We are fighting it and winning."

For the accuracy of the record it should be stated that Dr. Lang saw Mr. Stanley Baldwin five times just before the abdication. J. G. Lockhart, Lang's biographer, says Baldwin once specially sent for the Primate to consult him on a new proposal made by the King.

The remarks of Dr. Fisher infuriated some. The *Daily Express* said the Archbishop's immoderate language "cannot conceal the religious weakness of his case. The Archbishop asserts that the Princess has obeyed God's will. In fact she has obeyed the dogma of the Archbishop's own pamphlet. . . . His important admission will merely strengthen the belief that the romance was broken by ecclesiastical influence."

It was unfortunate that Dr. Fisher, if he was going to allow himself to be interviewed on the subject, did not state what happened when the Princess came to see him.

The sober liberal *News-Chronicle* commented: "No Christian who has studied the fearful effects of an unhappy and unsuccessful marriage, both on the parents and the children concerned, can afford to be complacent about the absolute sanctity of the marriage vows. Until the Church recognises and faces the implications of even this one simple fact, it risks cutting itself off from reality. And a Church that does that risks suffocation and decay."

Lord Beaverbrook's London *Evening Standard* said bluntly that Dr. Fisher's attitude "makes it inevitable that the question of disestablishment of the Church of England must be urgently examined."

Other newspapers, too, echoed this cry. But in Britain where nothing ever moves quickly—except in wartime—there was not going to be, nor has there been, an "urgent" examination of this kind. Nevertheless, some harm may have been done to the Church. In a second editorial, the *Manchester Guardian* concluded: "The one certain thing is that the British people are not really happy about the outcome of the affair, and some of the effects may be deep."

Although Princess Margaret in making her final decision did so primarily under the influence of Group Captain Townsend, she followed the dictates of the Church because she believes in its rules. There is no doubt about the genuineness of her religious feeling.

Throughout the week following the Princess' statement, the principals in the drama were mostly out of the public view. For two days after her announcement, the Princess remained secluded in Clarence House. Then London welcomed her back to the public life for which she was trained, as she fulfilled an engagement at St. Paul's Cathedral, where a commemorative service was being held for Dr. Barnardo's Homes. Men and women stood on chairs in the nave to watch her as she walked in.

When she left the Cathedral, some five hundred were gathered on the steps. They saw no royal faltering. When her face was caught for a few minutes in the floodlighting, she was seen to be smiling gently. There were no cheers, just a few calls of "Good luck" and "God bless you." Some women wept. It was raining.

In the House of Commons, the Prime Minister, Sir Anthony Eden, finally got around to answering Mr. Marcus Lipton, the Socialist member, who wanted to know if the Royal Marriage Act was to be amended or repealed. Eden admitted that "I have had this possibility very much in mind." No immediate legislation was contemplated. Eden thought he could take his time. A little over a year later he resigned. His successor, Mr. Harold Macmillan, probably prefers to leave the problem to another Prime Minister, perhaps a Socialist.

To the end, Peter Townsend remained discreet. He spent a few days at Uckfield House, where he had spent his last weekend with the Princess. He received reporters but said virtually nothing with his usual charm. He did say he would not be seeing the Princess again, but the reporters were uncertain whether he meant "never" or not before he returned to Brussels from his leave. They now know the answer.

With a chill rain spreading gloom over Lydd airport, Peter Townsend supervised the loading of his green Renault aboard an air freighter. Curious sightseers huddled nearby, but Peter had no last words for them, not even a farewell wave of the hand as he climbed aboard the plane. Half an hour later he was gone from England, bound for his air attaché post in Brussels.

The world thought the romance was over.

# The Epilogue
## July, 1958

Soon after dawn on may 24—empire day—1958, i said good-by to Peter Townsend as he left England for his fourth voluntary exile. He had spent the last night with me in Sussex, the only place in England where it had proved possible for him to live free from the press and public curiosity. The villagers of Paulborough fully respected his desire for privacy.

I do not think he will ever live permanently in England again. His visits in future will be brief. That is, unless circumstances change and he is free to marry the Princess.

When he left on May 24 he was sad but not bitter. His only immediate aim was to settle on the Continent and write the book which he has planned on his journey round the world. For that task he needed peace. He had not found it in England.

Peter has been accused of seeking publicity. As his friend, I can deny this. Yet, it is true that he has a habit of taking the dramatic course. Also he finds it impossible to tell a newspaperman a deliberate untruth. In consequence, he often appears to be publicizing himself. Basically he is a very shy and self-conscious man; this type of person seems always to attract publicity. I know that his happiest days since the crisis of 1955 were those when he was driving through Africa—days when he knew that he could not be reached or disturbed. In his make-up there is now something of the ascetic.

Forty-eight hours before Peter left England, this time for Belgium, this statement was issued from Buckingham Palace:

"The Press Secretary to the Queen is authorised to say that the report in the Tribune de Genève concerning a possible engagement between Princess Margaret and Group Captain

Peter Townsend is entirely untrue. Her Royal Highness's statement of 1955 remains unaltered."

The last sentence of this statement was significant. The words were almost identical with those used in the statement issued by Peter Townsend twenty-four hours after he arrived back in London from his eighty-week journey alone around the world.

The puzzled world may well ask: What do all these statements mean? What is their purport?

I think the time has come to reveal the facts about what has happened between Princess Margaret and Peter Townsend since they decided in the autumn of 1955 not to marry. The publication of the truth is in their best interests.

After the decision of 1955, one heard on all sides praise for the Princess who had been loyal to the teachings of the Church of England on marriage; loyal to the Queen her sister, and through her to the single family of many nations which the Queen represents; loyal to the Commonwealth. The *Times* said: "All the peoples of the Commonwealth will feel gratitude to her for taking the selfless, royal way which in their hearts they expected of her. They will pray and hope for her abiding happiness."

There was no word for Peter Townsend.

Princess Margaret and Peter Townsend were alone together for a few hours in Clarence House before the communiqué was issued on the evening of October 31, 1955. Before they parted, the Princess—according to friends of the royal family—pledged her undying love for Townsend and said that as she could not marry him she would never marry anyone else. Many might regard this as a statement made in a moment of great emotion and therefore not to be held as binding for all time. A statement that two persons do not intend to marry does not necessarily put an end to their love for one another.

When Margaret made her pledge never to marry anyone else, it was natural and chivalrous for Peter to be unwilling to accept it. His love for the Princess was no less than her love for him. At that moment he only wanted her to find happiness—abiding happiness, as the *Times* put it the next morning. So he told the Princess that it was his intention to remain away from England for at least two years. He expressed the hope that during this time she would meet someone whom she would wish to marry. If she did, it would make him happy if she found happiness.

And so Peter Townsend went back to his official duties in Brussels.

The next few months were the hardest days of his life. He was confronted with a difficult problem: should he remain on in the Air Force, or leave it and make a career in another sphere?

Peter was a man dedicated to the service of his country. It was the role of all his family. It was the role for which he himself had been trained. Therefore, to leave the RAF after twenty years was not an easy decision. And yet he was not completely in harmony with the postwar Air Force. He was a pilot of a past generation. Equally important, he had not been actively connected with the operational side of the Air Force since the war. He knew little about jets.

But if he left the Air Force what should he do? For a while he toyed with the idea of training race horses, a sport in which he had excelled as a gentleman rider during his years of exile in Brussels. And yet this idea did not quite offer him what he wanted.

The answer was not to come until the spring of 1956. He was on a visit to the Belgian Congo. One night on safari he thought, as he sat under a tropic African velvet sky, how much of the world he had not seen. From his pocket he took his diary and looked at a map of the globe. So was born the idea to drive round the world.

When he returned to Brussels he wrote me a note, suggesting that I should come over to see him and discuss the prospects of his writing about such a journey. At our first talk he explained that he had no desire to make an aimless journey. He wanted it, in fact, to be a job of work. To write about it seemed to him to be the answer. But he had doubts about his ability to write. What did I think?

I reminded him of his combat reports during the war, which I had read. I said that if he could write about his journey with the same dramatic sincerity with which he wrote about air fighting, he had nothing to fear.

At the end of a few days he had taken the final decision to make the journey and write about it. He set about planning it with all the enthusiasm with which he had led his squadron during the Battle of Britain. In fact, he planned the journey with the precision of a military operation. He worked out a timetable of eighty weeks to visit more than sixty countries. That was the timetable he carried out. In spite of all the hazards of the journey he arrived back in Brussels at the end of the 60,000-mile drive exactly on schedule.

It was natural that, as the time approached for Peter to start, the Princess should want to wish him farewell. In fact she herself was about to start on a journey to East Africa. They had a last—unreported—meeting at Clarence House on September 11, 1956. He went to lunch; they parted at about seven P.M. They were not to meet again for eighteen months.

The following day Peter flew back to Brussels. Three days later, on Sunday evening, I saw him off on his journey round the world.

If part of the purpose of that journey was to make these two people forget each other, then it had the very opposite effect, as nearly always happens when two people in love are separated. For the next eighteen months they no doubt wrote to each other. She would want to know about his adventures.

\*     \*     \*

After driving the 2,500 miles from Kano in Nigeria—including the perilous crossing of the Sahara Desert—Peter reached Algeria on Saturday, March 15, 1958. On Sunday afternoon I spoke to him from London on the telephone.

In letters it had been agreed that we should meet in Tangier, his intention being to complete his journey through Spain and France. But presumably because of his wish to reach London as soon as possible, he told me that he would cross direct to Marseilles and then drive straight to Brussels. He suggested that I fly to Algeria for "a talk."

I said that I would fly the next day if the French government would grant me a visa. At that time entry into Algeria was rather difficult for foreigners. However, through the kindness of the French Embassy in London and the French Prime Minister's office in Paris, the visa was granted, and by Tuesday evening I met Peter in the St. George Hotel, Algeria—the first time I had seen him since Brussels eighteen months before.

The man I shook hands with was very different man from the one I had bidden farewell. He was bronzed and fit; his eyes had a new alertness and there was a determination about him which I had not seen in him since those far-off days of the Battle of Britain. He was full of enthusiasm about the future.

As soon as we reached my room he wanted to know all the news from London. From questions that he put, it seemed to me that marriage between himself and the Princess was again in the air. He talked about the law and possible public reaction to the marriage. Only once did he mention the Church and that was in connection with Albert Schweitzer, whom he had been to see at Lambarene. And as the day went on it became more obvious that he was greatly under the influence of this Alsatian philosopher.

When Peter informed me that it was his intention to go to London as soon as he reached Brussels, I challenged the wisdom of such tactics. I said that in my opinion such a hasty visit would be misconstrued by many people; that it would spark off tremendous newspaper publicity, and that this in turn might be used by some in the Court against him and even against the Princess. He was not to be deterred.

During lunch the next day he revealed that he was sailing that night by a small ship to the port of Sete in Southern

France. It was an attempt to avoid the waiting newspapermen in Marseilles. The trick nearly succeeded. We got him aboard in secrecy. But a news agency correspondent discovered the next morning what had happened, and cabled a story to London. The reporters in Marseilles promptly packed their bags and departed for Sete. They were waiting on the dock when the ship arrived at dawn on Friday morning.

When I saw him off from Algiers that Wednesday evening, I promised to meet him on his arrival in London. The next day I flew home. On the flight I became more and more convinced that it would be harmful for Peter to fly to London as soon as he reached Brussels. Moreover, if he were to see the Princess in the following week, I realized that he would be doing so while the Queen was away. The Queen and Prince Philip were leaving London on Monday for a three-day State visit to Holland.

As soon as I arrived in London I telephoned Peter's lawyer and arranged to go down to Devonshire to see him on Saturday. He was on a few days' holiday. After a long talk he agreed with me that it could be unwise for Peter to come to London while the Queen was away, especially if he were to see the Princess. It would almost certainly be misinterpreted. We decided that he should try to dissuade Peter when he reached Brussels—probably the next day. In fact, Peter arrived there during the early hours of Monday morning.

The lawyer spoke to him on the telephone at the Astoria Hotel during the morning. Peter explained that his proposed meeting in London with the Princess had been arranged some days earlier. The date had been determined by the Princess' forthcoming visit to Germany, and by Peter's planned Easter holiday with his children. He understood that the Queen had been informed and that she did not object to the meeting's taking place while she was in Holland.

I met Peter on his arrival in London. He told me at once that he was to see the Princess that afternoon. Did I think he could get into Clarence House without being seen? I said that if he went in by the main gates, secrecy was impossible. I pointed out that he was already being followed by reporters and photographers. And it was my guess that already others were waiting outside Clarence House.

Although Fleet Street did not know the facts, intuition told the news editors what was the real purpose of Townsend's visit to London.

Peter's visit to Princess Margaret was timed for four o'clock. By two o'clock, when I drove along the Mall, the private road by the side of Clarence House was thronged with reporters and photographers. Presumably in an attempt to hide their identity, some were wearing dark suits and bowler hats—the civilian "uniform" of Guards officers from nearby Wellington Barracks.

About three-thirty Peter drove from his lawyer's office in Lincoln's Inn to the Rover Company's showroom in Piccadilly. He was followed all the way by newspapermen on motorcycles or in cars. It was now quite obvious that his visit to Clarence House—the first since the autumn of 1955, so far as the press knew—would be known and widely publicized.

Peter spoke to the Princess shortly before four o'clock and it was decided that the visit should take place, whatever the repercussions.

Promptly at four o'clock Peter was driven by his chauffeur in his green Rover limousine through the double black gates of Clarence House. Within minutes, the London *Evening Standard* was selling in St. James's, with the banner headline: THEY'RE TOGETHER AGAIN.

What transpired between the couple at this first meeting in eighteen months can only be a matter of conjecture. But I do not think that the question of marriage was discussed. They had too much else to talk about. In a sense, they had to get to know each other all over again. And this meeting was to be the first of many, if the plans of the Princess and Townsend were to work out smoothly. Anyway, it was a very happy reunion, as was evident from the smiling photographs that night of the Princess at a film première of *A Farewell to Arms*.

It had been the intention of Peter to spend the night with me in the country, and so that I could get him out of London without being seen I had transferred his luggage at lunchtime from his car to my Hillman. We had arranged to rendezvous after he left Clarence House at Whitehall Court in Westminster—a block of luxury flats and clubs, where Peter had often stayed when in London for brief visits during his exile. This building has the great advantage of several exits. But on this evening they were of no avail. When he drove from Clarence House at about six thirty, he was again pursued by a horde of pressmen. Escape from Whitehall Court unnoticed proved impossible, so we decided to stay there the night. In fact, we stayed there for thirty-six nightmare hours. The building was virtually surrounded by newspapermen day and night, watching in eight-hour shifts.

The London newspapers the next morning were a shock to the Princess and Peter, but they proved an even greater shock to the royal family and the Court officials.

During the morning Peter spoke to the Princess on the telephone, and then drove to see his lawyer. It had been agreed that Peter, the lawyer, and I should lunch together. At lunch they asked me if I thought a statement from Peter would stop the press publicity. I had to say frankly that in my opinion it would not. This was a story too big for the world's newspapers to abandon lightly. However, a statement could do no harm. So I sat at my typewriter and wrote (after much discussion) the twenty-nine words which were issued by Peter's lawyer to the Press Association at three o'clock— one hour before it had been planned for Peter to go again to Clarence House.

This statement said:

> There are no grounds whatever for supposing that my seeing Princess Margaret in any way alters the situation declared specifically in the Princess' statement in the autumn of 1955.

The purpose was to quiet the press, to placate those Court officials who were hostile to Peter's seeing Margaret, and to remind the world of the Princess' decision of 1955.

It must be remembered that the Queen, Prince Philip, and senior members of the Court were all away in Holland. When they saw the London newspapers, with their front pages containing practically no other news, there was something bordering on panic and there were hasty telephone calls to London.

The previous night in The Hague, a Court spokesman had told English reporters accompanying the Queen that Her Majesty knew before she left London that Townsend would be seeing her sister. But what officials said "on the record" and what they said "off the record" were very different stories. The burden of the statements "off the record" was that the Queen did *not* know and that both the Princess and Townsend were being "stubborn" and "naughty."

What was going on in The Hague had immediate repercussions in London. Peter left Whitehall Court soon after three thirty on Thursday afternoon. He was making one brief call and then driving to Clarence House; when he spoke to the Princess on the telephone a few minutes before four o'clock to ensure that the gates were open so that he could drive in without being photographed, he was astonished to learn that the visit was "off." The Princess told him that she felt that it would be wiser not to meet again until the Queen returned to London. That night he sent her four dozen red roses.

The Princess was to leave London the next day on a two-day visit to Germany. At dinner that evening Peter felt that it was better he should leave London immediately and visit his mother in Somerset. But he considered it important, for the sake of his mother whose health was none too good, that the journey should be made in secrecy. This was not easy. He was still virtually a prisoner in the building.

After dark I did a little planning. I moved my car to a side street where there was an exit from Whitehall Court, which we had previously decided to use as a last resort. Also, I had noticed that the reporters staying all night were relieved at six o'clock in the morning, so that for a few minutes the watch was relaxed a little while gossip was exchanged. We decided that this was the best moment to make our escape. And it worked exactly as we planned.

As a sad-eyed Princess, wearing one of Peter's roses, flew off to Germany, I was driving Peter across the south of England to his mother. But our problems were not all over. From a telephone call we knew that there were many newspapermen and photographers in Stogumber, where Peter's mother has a thatched cottage, and also in Bicknoller, where Peter's sister, Stephanie, lives.

For the remainder of our journey we discussed the best way of getting into Stephanie's cottage without being seen. In the end we decided to do a reconnaissance when we arrived. In fact, we drove through both villages, Stogumber and Bicknoller. Although we had to run the gantlet of the watching pressmen, none of them spotted Peter sitting beside me. They took us for newspapermen—which, I suppose, was not a completely inaccurate judgment. However, it was obviously impossible to get into Stephanie's cottage by the front door without being seen. In the end Peter got in unnoticed through the back by going through several people's gardens. He remained in the house without going out until Sunday morning. And no one knew whether he was there or not.

Friday, March 28, I shall always feel was a vital day in the affairs of Peter and Margaret.

From The Hague, the American Associated Press Correspondent had cabled a story which was reprinted the next day as a lead item by the London *Daily Express*. Under seven-column headlines: Palace and the Princess, "The Queen Was Irked" by That Tea Party, the story read:

> "A pensive Queen Elizabeth tonight ended her three-day state visit to Holland—a visit suddenly overshadowed by Princess Margaret's tea-party meeting with Group Captain Peter Townsend.

"And as the Queen and the Duke of Edinburgh boarded the Royal yacht *Britannia* for Britain, Commander Richard Colville, the Queen's Press Secretary, refused to discuss the reunion between the beautiful Princess and the Battle of Britain hero. He described the meeting as 'no mystery.'

"But despite lack of official comment, reporters close to Palace circles received the strong impression that the Queen was *irked*—irked because the handsome Group Captain and the Princess had renewed their friendship after more than two years . . . and while she was out of the country on a state visit to a foreign nation.

"It is an almost 'open secret' in Holland that people close to the Queen regard the couple's resumption of friendship—in the Queen's absence—as perversity on the part of the Princess and her former suitor.

"Reports here say that the globe-trotter insisted on seeing the Princess and that Princess Margaret fell in with the idea."

The story was grossly unfair to the Princess, and particularly unfair—by suggesting that he had forced Margaret into meeting him—to Townsend.

On Friday morning, only the Labour Party's *Daily Herald* had a sympathetic word. In an editorial, this newspaper stated:

". . . To the astonishment of numerous fogies, the friendship of the Princess and Group Captain Townsend still goes on. *Publicly, proudly, and without regard to fogies.*

"Millions will applaud. The Princess gives an example of the modern way of behaving, in the good sense of that word. It is courteous, pleasant and civilised.

"Group Captain Townsend . . . had suffered much through no fault of his. He has borne himself well. It is right that the tittle-tattling world should be shown how the Princess values his friendship.

"She made it clear in 1955 that her reason for renouncing a marriage was in accordance with the teaching of the Church. . . . We say only, as we said then, that few people could blame the Princess if one day she did change her mind."

It was perhaps premature of the *Daily Herald* to suggest that Margaret might one day change her mind. In my opinion the position between the couple at that moment was clear: they wanted to be friends, free to see each other when they wished, free to discuss and plan their future. Was that asking too much? they wondered.

On Sunday I drove Peter from Somerset to stay with a friend in Berkshire. The Princess flew back to England from Germany in the afternoon and went straight to Royal Lodge, Windsor, where she usually stays with her mother at weekends. The Queen drove over from the Castle and had tea with her.

Immediately after tea Margaret telephoned Peter and told him that she had been persuaded not to see him again during this visit to England, but that the Queen had agreed to the principle of future meetings. They talked for nearly an hour.

The next morning Peter and I drove to London. That evening, almost unobserved, Peter flew back to Brussels.

It would be surprising if he did not feel hurt by the reactions of officials at the Court. I have seen copies of several "off the record" statements given by officials who were with the Queen at The Hague. They make interesting reading. In every instance they are critical not only of Peter Townsend, but also, by implication, of Princess Margaret.

Alan Dick of the *Daily Herald* wrote from Rotterdam that the Court officials attending on the Queen were saying that the Princess showed "indifference" to her sister's position by keeping—and making public—an engagement which could easily have been postponed for a week; and that the Queen had been "acutely embarrassed by a situation created while her back was turned."

Alan Dick added that an official said: "Townsend and the Princess have been parted for more than two years. Another two days could not have made much difference."

*    *    *

Peter, back in Brussels, waited a few days for his sons, Giles and Hugo, to join him for their Easter holidays. They went off to Spain for two weeks, had a wonderful time free from press inquisitiveness, but then had it marred by the publicity caused by the theft of Peter's suitcase from his car on their last night in Paris.

They traveled to England on Sunday, and after Peter had delivered the boys safely back to their mother near Sevenoaks in Kent he joined me in Sussex.

The timing of his return to England this time was deliberate. The Princess was still away on her triumphal tour of the Caribbean. She was not due back in London until the following Wednesday. This enabled Peter to move about in comparative freedom.

On the evening of his return we talked long over dinner about the future and where it would be best for him to live. He wanted to stay in England where he would be near the Princess and so, he felt, be free to meet her whenever they wished without undue publicity. He saw no reason why, for example, he should not take her to a theater or a public restaurant. As he put it, other escorts did so without criticism. Why shouldn't he?

I said that it was necessary for everyone to get used to seeing him around and for him to be allowed to merge into the landscape. Meanwhile, I thought the most favorable place for him to live was with his mother in Somerset. He had his book to write, which would take him six months. This book is more important than just writing any book. It is the key, in Peter's opinion, to his future career. His writings during the journey have given him a taste for writing. He believes, and others share this view, that he has a talent for it. It would in many ways be an ideal career for him. It would enable him to travel, which he adores. But, perhaps more important, it would permit a new and firmer relationship between him and the Princess. Perhaps one of the severest criticisms leveled against him in 1955 when seeking marriage with Margaret, was that he was a man without a career. It was almost the old-fashioned Victorian criticism: How is he going to support the girl?

Peter agreed with me that perhaps Stogumber, nestling under the Quantock Hills in Somerset—scene of so many happy days during his childhood—was the most suitable retreat for him to do his writing in. He also agreed that it would be unwise to see the Princess at Clarence House as soon as she returned.

So a day or so later he went off to his mother. From Somerset he had talks on the telephone with the Princess after her homecoming and she invited him to lunch with her and friends on Sunday at Royal Lodge, Windsor Park. This he did—without any newspaper's knowing it.

After lunch he went back to Somerset.

A week went by without another meeting being arranged. The couple then decided to try one at Clarence House and see if it could take place without publicity. It was arranged for six o'clock on Monday.

But once again the news leaked out. And I regret to say that it was all my fault, although, of course, unwittingly.

This is how it happened. Peter had spent the night with me in the country and on Monday morning we had driven to London. We had lunched with a friend.

About five o'clock Peter suggested that I walk around Clarence House at five-thirty and insure that there were no reporters about. This I did and telephoned him at five-forty-five that everything was all right. I then came out of the callbox in St. James's and walked back to the Mall and into St. James's Park. Unfortunately just as I was emerging from the private road by Clarence House into the Mall someone connected with the *Daily Express* was passing in a car and saw me. I didn't see him. He put two and two together and in consequence his office sent a reporter to see what was happening.

All the newspapers printed big stories on the following morning, the Queen's Press Secretary having confirmed at midnight that Townsend had called on the Princess earlier in the evening.

Fleet Street was now fully alerted, and Peter began to have doubts about the wisdom of remaining in England. As he bluntly put it: "They will never leave me alone. I cannot write under such conditions."

That he and the Princess wanted to continue their friendship there is no doubt. If they discussed marriage they could obviously reach no definite conclusions.

I think an important new element had entered into the matter. Peter realized that the Princess was fulfilling her role splendidly. The Caribbean tour had proved that. People were talking of her as "Britain's Ambassadress" in the same way as they had talked thirty years earlier of the Prince of Wales. If she married him, how could she give all this up? Perhaps they wondered whether she would have to give up her royal status. What would happen if she put the problem into the lap of Parliament? After all, the law only required her to give the Privy Council one year's notice of her intention to marry. True, either the House of Lords or the House of Commons could within that year veto the marriage. But would either House do so?

Peter went to Clarence House on Tuesday evening with his mind made up. Any question of marriage would have to wait until he had finished his book in the autumn: meanwhile he must have complete freedom to see the Princess when and where he wished.

But the publicity in the newspapers that morning had aroused all the same reactions as before in the Court. During the day new pressures were brought to bear on Margaret.

When Peter went to Clarence House that evening his entrance was seen. Fleet Street were taking no more chances. Reporters of both the *Daily Mail* and the *Daily Express* were outside.

At seven-thirty Peter left, this time by another gate to avoid the waiting reporters.

Again the couple were dogged by bad luck, and this time partly because of Peter's tactics. By going out by a different gate from that by which he had entered Clarence House, he led the reporters to think that he was still there and presumably staying to dinner.

About nine-thirty they wanted to write their stories for the first editions which go to press about ten-thirty. When these were printed and available to newspapers in Fleet Street, the Press Association—the big English news agency—sent a reporter up to Clarence House. It was then about eleven-thirty. So far as everyone knew, Peter was still with the Princess.

At twelve-twenty a Rover saloon came out of the main gates of Clarence House, driven by a man. The reporters, who could not see too clearly in the dark, assumed it was Townsend. They reported his departure to their offices.

The next morning, Wednesday, there were front-page stories in all newspapers, under headlines: "Peter Dines with the Princess."

But in the *Tribune de Genève,* an important Continental newspaper, there was a story even more embarrassing to the Palace. This newspaper's London correspondent stated: "An engagement may be announced soon." And then went on:

> "Everything looks as if it was intended to prepare the general public for the announcement.
> "It is also understood that Queen Elizabeth no longer has any objection. . . ."

It is a tradition of Buckingham Palace not to deny newspaper reports. But, as I have said, the Princess was already under great pressure. This story, published in Switzerland and cabled back to London, provided the Palace with an excuse to act.

At midday on Wednesday, the Queen drove across from Buckingham Palace to Clarence House to see her sister. Princess Margaret did not resist her sister's proposal that an official denial—an unprecedented act—be made of the *Tribune de Genève* story. That evening the following statement was issued from Buckingham Palace:

> "The Press Secretary to the Queen is authorised to say that the report in the *Tribune de Genève* concerning a possible engagement between Princess Margaret and Group Captain Peter Townsend is entirely untrue.
>
> "Her Royal Highness's statement of 1955 remains unaltered."

This statement did not say that the friendship was at an end. Nor did it entirely rule out the possibility of marriage at a future date.

My belief is that Princess Margaret would still like to marry Peter Townsend. And it would seem that while there is hope the couple are prepared to wait.

Before the statement was issued from Buckingham Palace the Princess telephoned the text to Peter, who was then back in Somerset with his mother. He agreed that it was in their best interests that it should be issued. But he felt more strongly than ever that it would be better for them both if he went back to the Continent to write his book. The Princess could only agree.

On Friday Peter drove from Somerset and spent the night with me in Sussex. The next morning, at dawn, we said goodby as he set out for Brussels—his fourth voluntary exile. In his suitcase was a new photograph of the Princess, which she had given him at their last meeting on Tuesday evening.

The reader, quite naturally, will ask: what of the future? This much I can say: they would like to marry, but at the moment the religious and political issues remain insurmountable. While they exist, there can be *no* marriage. Nor will they try to circumvent them by any form of subterfuge. The Princess has already shown that she understands her duty. But there could be changes in the future affecting both their lives, and these changes could make marriage between them possible.

For the present I think that the Princess and Townsend are

only anxious that their love and friendship should be established in such a way that it is accepted by the Court, the Church, Parliament and the public. This can be achieved only by the people becoming accustomed to the idea slowly. At a later stage the couple could be seen together even at events patronized by Royalty.

So, during the next few months, there may be occasional visits by Townsend to England to see the Princess. He did not go to London to wish her farewell before her Canadian tour because they both felt it would start a new spate of publicity.

The real key to Peter's future lies, I believe, in the completion of his book at the end of this year. It is planned for publication in the Autumn of 1959. Although it will be based on his journey around the world, it will at the same time have a strong philosophic and perhaps political content. For these reasons—and I have seen the synopsis—it may have an important impact, and so establish Peter as a new writer. If that proves to be the case, then the position of his friendship with the Princess and her family will be more strongly established.

This fact, however, must be faced: Princess Margaret and Peter Townsend are deeply in love, and their love has survived all the vicissitudes of publicity and separation.

I am therefore tempted to put the question: if the Princess decided in the future to marry Townsend and sent a formal indication of her intention to the Privy Council, as now required under the provision of the Royal Marriages Act of 1772, would Parliament use its authority under the Act to veto such a marital union? For my part, I do not think so, nor do I accept the view advanced in 1955 that if such a marriage took place it would be necessary for the Princess to renounce her Royal status and her State income.

The story of Princess Margaret and Peter Townsend is not yet ended. In fairy stories the gallant knight slays the dragon, rescues the Princess, marries her, and they live happily for ever after.